TOP NEW ZEALAND
DIVE SITES

GILLIAN and DARRYL TORCKLER

RAUPO

A RAUPO BOOK
Published by the Penguin Group
Penguin Group (NZ), 67 Apollo Drive, Rosedale,
North Shore 0632, New Zealand (a division of Pearson New Zealand Ltd)
Penguin Group (USA) Inc., 375 Hudson Street,
New York, New York 10014, USA
Penguin Group (Canada), 90 Eglinton Avenue East, Suite 700, Toronto,
Ontario, M4P 2Y3, Canada (a division of Pearson Penguin Canada Inc.)
Penguin Books Ltd, 80 Strand, London, WC2R 0RL, England
Penguin Ireland, 25 St Stephen's Green,
Dublin 2, Ireland (a division of Penguin Books Ltd)
Penguin Group (Australia), 250 Camberwell Road, Camberwell,
Victoria 3124, Australia (a division of Pearson Australia Group Pty Ltd)
Penguin Books India Pvt Ltd, 11, Community Centre,
Panchsheel Park, New Delhi – 110 017, India
Penguin Books (South Africa) (Pty) Ltd, 24 Sturdee Avenue,
Rosebank, Johannesburg 2196, South Africa

Penguin Books Ltd, Registered Offices: 80 Strand, London, WC2R 0RL, England

First published by Penguin Group (NZ), 2008
1 3 5 7 9 10 8 6 4 2

Typeset by IslandBridge
Maps by Outline Draughting and Graphics Ltd
Printed by Everbest Printing Co. Ltd, China

ISBN 9780143010098

A catalogue record for this book is available
from the National Library of New Zealand.

www.penguin.co.nz

Contents

Introduction

After decades of diving around the globe, we still experience a thrill whenever we enter New Zealand's underwater world. Each dive is a journey of perpetual discovery: of new species and old favourites; of new locations and different seasons. The discovery, and rediscovery, of creatures remains for us one of the true highlights of diving, and New Zealand never lets us down. Once the bubbles have settled, we watch shimmering schools of fish gliding amid clear waters, through archways and into dark caverns.

Each dive is preceded by anticipation and expectations. And every dive is rewarding and exciting: the sighting of a rare fish, a sunfish, a manta-ray or perhaps even a whale shark. It might be the appearance of old favourites – snapper or blue maomao. Although the swimming creatures capture our attention, closer inspection reveals reefs and underwater walls encrusted with colourful sponges, invertebrates and algae.

New Zealand – a group of islands at the bottom of the world – is surrounded by vast oceans on all sides, but this was not so 140 million years ago. Then, New Zealand was attached to the vast supercontinent of Gondwana, which included Australia, Africa, Antarctica and South America. What started as a slow subterranean drift apart has resulted in total isolation. The underground tectonic plate activity, along with sculpting by glaciers, has created a land of exquisite diversity: steep mountains, majestic volcanoes and cavernous valleys abound. New Zealand's landmass is neither flat nor even and the clashing of the Pacific and Indo-Australian plate results in the ever-present geothermal activity and rumblings. Cone-shaped volcanoes dot the North Island and steam seeps

Dusky Sound

intermittently from hillsides. The South Island's western mountain ranges are the result of a constant underground battle – each day the mountains edge a little higher as the tectonic plates collide.

The underwater terrain is equally unique. Forced rock movements and volcanic eruptions have left their mark here, as well. The now submerged sea floor is convoluted: ridges, reefs and pinnacles are home to many different species, enticing the underwater explorer. Deeper still, a network of some of the world's longest underwater canyons and trenches support deep-dwelling underwater life, such as sperm whales and giant squid.

When New Zealand separated from Gondwana, the isolation of flora and fauna commenced, and today there are no snakes and only a few mammals. The land boasts a large number of endemic species but mammals are rare – only bats and sea mammals occur naturally. New Zealand fur seals were nearly hunted to extinction during the late nineteenth century, but today they bask fearlessly on rocks around the South Island and the west coast of the North Island. Seals share the oceanic waters with other marine mammals. Dolphins will often swim alongside boats as they traverse the offshore waterways, while many species of whales are sighted from boats. Some, such as orca and sperm whales, are resident here. Others, such as southern right and humpback whales, pass through on their migratory pathways. Kaikoura is one of the few places in the world where you might be diving with seals in the morning, snorkelling with dolphins in the afternoon, and watching magnificent whales surface in the deep-blue water in between.

Although the marine animals are the largest and perhaps most visible of New Zealand's abundant underwater marine life, thousands of species of fish, algae, invertebrates and other creatures make their home around the coast. Among them are over 800 species of algae, 250 species of reef fish and 70 different sea urchins. As a result, divers are rarely disappointed when they venture beneath New Zealand's seas.

White Island

Kapiti Island

Diving in New Zealand

New Zealand's islands extend through a wide latitude range and are surrounded by two main bodies of water: the feisty Tasman Sea to the west, and the vast Pacific Ocean to the north, east and south. These seas offer unique underwater environments and are home to equally unique animals. Diving in New Zealand is mostly classified as temperate: but the northernmost island group, the Kermadec Islands, has a tropical feel underwater; the northeast coast of the North Island a subtropical feel at times; while the southernmost islands, in what is sometimes called the roaring Southern Ocean, are exposed to sub-Antarctic conditions.

This results in a strange mix of marine creatures around the coastline, and is exaggerated when the East Auckland Current, which sweeps past the North Island, occasionally brings a stray sea turtle or whale shark with it. Even without these rare sightings, most people are impressed with both the diversity and number of fishes they encounter underwater in New Zealand. And with each passing year, this is amplified by a unique system of marine reserves and parks around the coastline.

New Zealand's first marine reserve, Cape Rodney-Okarari Point Marine Reserve, locally known as Goat Island Bay, was established in 1975 and has become the flagship of the marine reserve movement. By 2007, more than 30 additional marine reserves had been established, with more under consideration. Encouragingly, all of the reserves boast higher fish numbers

Introduction

than their neighbouring underwater environs thanks to the implementation of a full no-take policy.

Nearly 88 per cent of New Zealand territorial waters are now fully protected. But 99 per cent of those waters are located far offshore – around the Auckland and Kermadec Island groups. The transformation and protection of New Zealand waters is a continual process and, ultimately, many New Zealanders would like to see 10 per cent of the coastline of their three main islands protected.

In the north, the Poor Knights Islands, also designated a full marine reserve, are one of New Zealand's best-known dive locations. The vast underwater arches and caves found here are themselves astoundingly beautiful, but when a school of stingrays or blue maomao pass by the effect is pure magic. Northland, the gateway to Poor Knights' is also home to a network of scuttled ships that are now fully established artificial reefs. The most famous of these – the *Rainbow Warrior* – was a Greenpeace protest vessel blown up by agents of the French Government while at dock in Auckland Harbour. Of course, there are other 'real shipwrecks' scattered around the coast, often in deep water and typically not in the easiest of dive locations. One of the best known of these is the *Mikhail Lermontov*, a Russian cruise ship that sank in 1986 after hitting rocks near Cape Jackson in Cook Strait.

Alderman Islands

Nestled in the southwest corner of New Zealand is the World Heritage listed Fiordland National Park, which is part of the Te W hipounamu Southwest New Zealand World Heritage Area. Most of this park and its fiords, which encompasses over 1.2 million hectares of pristine forest, remains almost completely inaccessible by road. Fiordland is one of New Zealand's most visited locations, but very few of the hundreds of daily visitors venture underwater. Those that do are not disappointed. The

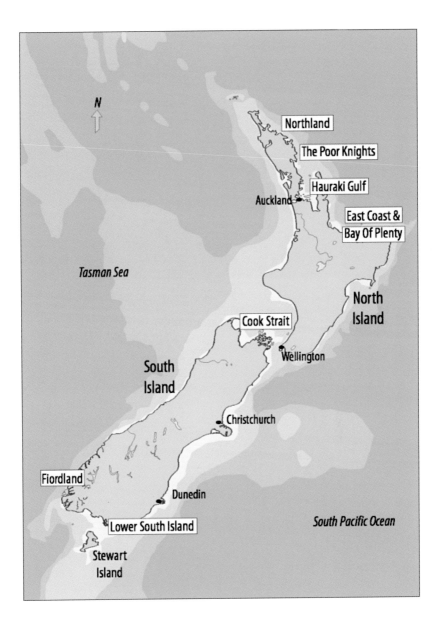

N

Northland

The Poor Knights

Hauraki Gulf

Auckland

East Coast &
Bay Of Plenty

Tasman Sea

North
Island

Cook Strait

Wellington

South
Island

Christchurch

Fiordland

Dunedin

Lower South Island

South Pacific Ocean

Stewart
Island

Marlborough Sounds

unique underwater geology of the fiords has created a serene underwater environment where rare black coral and other deep species thrive in fairly shallow water.

Between these two extremes of the country, the diving is equally diverse. You can dive on an active volcano in the Bay of Plenty, swim with wild seals and dolphins off the Kaikoura coast, or explore a sunken passenger liner in Cook Strait. Or perhaps a decommissioned New Zealand Navy vessel is more to your taste? Whether you seek spectacular underwater geology, love diving on submerged ships, or simply like to admire marine life in its natural habitat, New Zealand has plenty to offer almost every diver. Come with us as we introduce you to some of our favourite dive sites around the coast of New Zealand.

Choosing the sites

What defines a top dive site? It might be a favourite first dive, a special cave or shipwreck, or just a place that is teeming with more life than you have ever seen. It might be a place that stimulates your senses or evokes emotions. Choosing just a handful of locations is no easy task. There is little doubt that if one was to dive and explore all of New Zealand's

15,000-kilometre coastline, numerous additional 'top dive sites' would be identified, each offering unique diving experiences.

The dives featured in this book are not the deepest; the most famous wrecks; the most visited dive locations; or the sites with the best underwater visibility. But each dive offers a unique underwater experience. We are certain our choices will leave some people protesting. We will undoubtedly have omitted a favourite cray hole, or a beloved shipwreck. We simply could not include every dive site and have had to make some hard decisions about what to leave out. The dive sites featured are a mix of those that are unique to New Zealand; or contain unique shipwrecks; or have interesting underwater architecture or geology; or are simply home to interesting or plentiful wildlife. We considered the quantity of fish and other animals, rarity of certain species, historical nature of the sites, underwater visibility and accessibility.

All of the dives are accessible, either by beach or regular charter boat operations. This last proviso sadly excluded a few of our very favourite dive sites. Some of these are isolated pinnacles, reefs or sea mounts, while many others are located in the Three Kings and Kermadec Islands, and remote areas of Fiordland. The dives that are included are varied and accessible, and every one of them has left a strong impression on us. Check them out – we don't think you'll be disappointed.

Take care

Diving anywhere is a hazardous activity, and New Zealand is no different to any other country. Fortunately, New Zealand doesn't have many dangerous underwater creatures. Blue and mako sharks do live in the deep waters of the coast, but divers rarely see them. Occasionally, great whites are seen around southern shores and, in summer months, bronze whalers are

The *Rainbow Warrior*

often seen in shallower waters off northern coasts. You need to heed usual diving safety rules, keep an eye on bottom time, and remember you will be diving in remote areas far from advanced medical care.

Coastal diving in New Zealand comes with its own risks, including surge, limited underwater visibility and kelp. Consult with tide charts and local weather predictions to avoid diving in large swells, or at inappropriate tidal intervals. Local knowledge is invaluable for choosing the optimal tidal times to enjoy easy access and great diving.

Diving conditions

Water temperature varies greatly from the north to the south. In the summer months (December–February), water temperatures off the northeast coast of the North Island are likely to be around 20°C, compared with 12–15°C around Stewart Island in the south. Expect winter temperatures (June–August) to be about five to six degrees lower. New Zealand has a relatively small tidal range of 1–3 m but, as in most countries, coastal diving is hampered by water run-off from the land, especially after rain. Also, algal or plankton blooms are a seasonal challenge, affecting visibility in spring and early summer. Consult local dive operators, look into local weather and sea forecasts, and take tidal and swell conditions into account when planning to dive or snorkel. Diving in New Zealand is restricted to those holding recognised diving certification.

Marlborough Sounds

Access to dive sites

Most sites featured have operators, who regularly dive these locations, offering trips to them (see pages 173–74 for diving websites and current operators). Many of the dives are located offshore and therefore need to be accessed by charter boat. The local dive operators understand their area best – they'll know the best (and worst) times to visit their local dive sites. Always take an underwater torch with you to investigate inside caves, wrecks, and nooks and crannies, as well as to illuminate the colourful walls and creatures.

The *Tui*

Using this book

The dive sites in this book are grouped by geographic regions from north to south. Each location features:

- an introduction to the area

- our choice of the best dives

- information for planning each dive, for example, minimum and maximum depth, sea conditions, terrain, level of experience

- a detailed description of what to expect underwater

- photographs of the sites and some of the animals you might find there.

Two areas have so much to offer divers that they deserve special treatment. So, the Poor Knights Islands has a chapter to itself, rather than being included in the Northland chapter; similarly, Fiordland National Park has been separated from the chapter on the South Island.

A photographic species guide (pages 165–72) is included to help you identify some of the fish, animals and algae you will encounter.

Northland

The northernmost and warmest part of New Zealand is one of the country's most visited places, with the Bay of Islands often the first stop on many present-day travellers' itineraries. In fact, it has always been the case. According to Maori legend, when explorer Kupe travelled across the oceans from his ancestral homeland of Hawaiki, he first set foot in Northland – on the tail of the legendary fish that his ancestor Maui had fished from the ocean with his magic hook.

European explorers were also drawn to the area, and its importance was recognised when the Treaty of Waitangi was signed between Governor William Hobson and Maori chiefs at Waitangi in the Bay of Islands. Across the water, the township of Russell was the first commercial centre of New Zealand. In fact, it was New Zealand's first capital city, before William Hobson moved the capital to Auckland in 1840. In those early days, the Bay of Islands was frequently visited by whaling ships. Today, the bay is as popular as ever – but now the visitors are tourists. And many take to the water.

Many of New Zealand's best dive locations are located here. Most divers prefer water that is warm and clear, and the water around Northland is both. But this is also where marine life is plentiful. This is the gateway to two fabulous offshore island groups: the Three Kings Islands and the Poor Knights Islands. Unfortunately, there are no regular trips to the uninhabited and rarely visited Three Kings, the final home of the *Elingamite*, a passenger steamer. Divers are also attracted to the Three Kings for their underwater caves and abundance of marine life. The water literally boils with the motion and frenzy of many sea birds and fish.

The Poor Knights (covered in the next chapter) are undoubtedly the premier dive location of New Zealand and the perfect place to start your

The wreck of the *Elingamite*

West King Island in the Three Kings Islands group is the final resting ground of the *Elingamite*, which sank in November 1902 when it hit incorrectly charted islands early one foggy morning, killing 45 of the 194 people aboard. The ship was carrying 1.5 tons of gold bullion and silver coins from Sydney to Auckland. The wreck, which lies 38 m deep, was salvaged by two of New Zealand's great diving pioneers – Kelly Tarlton and Wade Doak.

Northland diving adventure, but don't stop there. Northland is also the home of four scuttled ships – HMNZS *Canterbury*, the *Rainbow Warrior*, HMNZS *Tui* and HMNZS *Waikato*. All were sunk off the eastern coast in order to make artificial reefs for divers.

The Cavalli Islands, the final resting site of the *Rainbow Warrior*, consists of one large island (Motukawanui) and many smaller islands, about 5 km offshore from Matauri Bay. Captain James Cook named the islands Cavalle after buying some fish of the same name from the local Maori inhabitants. Those fish may have been common trevally, a fish once so plentiful here that the sea surface was almost a solid wall of silvery scales at times.

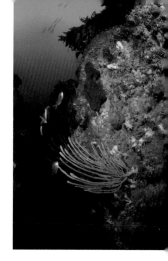

Cavalli Islands

Northland's long coastline is easily accessed, and there are many offshore islands and sheltered bays to explore. On the west coast, long beaches take the brunt of the Tasman Sea, and make diving difficult. On the eastern coast, the prevailing seas and swells are usually calm enough to dive or snorkel off almost any bay or beach. The diving here is limitless.

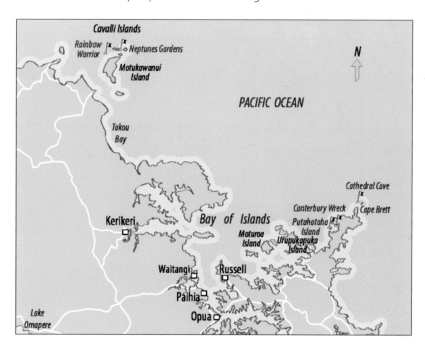

Diving in Northland

You can snorkel or shore-dive from much of the east coast of Northland, or take charter boats to the offshore island groups. The underwater visibility will vary greatly, depending on where you dive. Expect 8–15 m, with clearer water as you head further offshore. The visibility is not so dependent on water temperature and the waters are more fishy during the summer months, especially January and February. Northland benefits from the warm East Auckland Current that sweeps through the area. Water temperature ranges from 15–16°C (59–60°F) during May to September) to 20–23°C (68–73°F) between January and April.

The *Canterbury* wreck

Cathedral Cave

Location	Piercy Island, Bay of Islands
Access	Boat
Type of dive	Reef, cave
Level	Advanced
Snorkel	No
Depth range	0–40+ m
When to dive	Calm conditions; not in northerly or easterly conditions
Current	Slight in the cave; can be strong outside of cave
Look for	Lord Howe coral fish, moray eels, interesting rock formations

Piercy Island, at the outer edge of the Bay of Islands, is a busy location. Each day, boats take tourists there to marvel at the natural rock sculpture, especially the famous 'hole in the rock', a giant archway large enough to drive a big boat through. Nearby Cathedral Cave is similar, but a true cave.

Both are probably blister caves of volcanic origin. Cathedral Cave's tall triangular entrance leads you into a large, wedge-shaped cave. The underwater walls of the cave plunge vertically and large boulders are scattered across the sea floor, which slopes from about 15 m at the back of the cave to 35 m at its entrance. The cave walls are lined with anemones and sponges; and the boulder landscape is the busy home territory of red moki, Lord Howe coral fish, marblefish and leatherjackets. About halfway along the left side of the cave is a deep vertical crack that is filled with bigeyes and the occasional splendid perch.

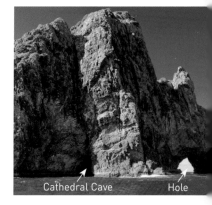

Cathedral Cave   Hole

Swimming out of the cave, follow the wall to the right, which rims a large rocky shelf. The wall has interesting ledges to explore and will lead you to an intriguing rock formation – a vertical wall resembling a pancake stack. Each 'pancake' edge is coated with colourful sponges and anemones, while invertebrates, eels and fish snuggle into the indentations between.

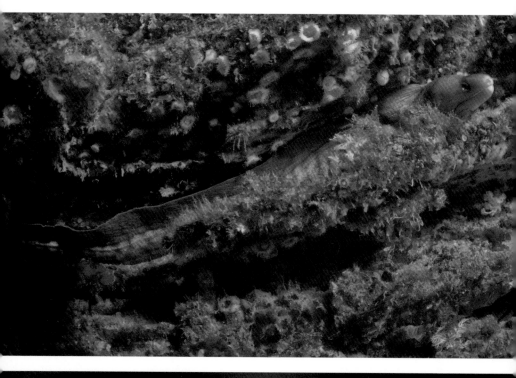

The *Canterbury*

Location	Deepwater Cove, Bay of Islands
Access	Boat
Type of dive	Wreck
Level	Advanced or experienced open water
Snorkel	No
Depth range	12–38 m
When to dive	Anytime
Current	Slight, but can be stronger on spring tides
Look for	Jewel anemones, ship's gear and equipment

The *Canterbury*, a Royal New Zealand Navy frigate, was commissioned in 1971. After 34 years of naval service, it was decommissioned and scuttled at Deepwater Cove, near the entrance to the Bay of Islands, in November 2007. It is the fourth and newest addition to the chain of recreational shipwrecks along the Northland coast. She is lying in pristine condition almost upright on the sandy sea floor. We had never before had the opportunity to dive a wreck that we have previously been aboard when she was afloat. It is surreal to float in the control room of the bridge, where we previously talked with the ship's captain; or to hover inside the helicopter hangar where a 30-year-old helicopter sat before jauntily taking to the skies above the coral-fringed Pacific Island of Niue.

As you descend, you reach the deck structures about 20 m or so, but the sheer bulk of this ship – 113 m long – means you can't see from one end to the other. The ship's stern sits on the sandy sea floor at 38 m, so bottom time is always going to be limited even if you head straight down. You need to plan many dives on this wreck to really experience the whole ship. In the few short months since the ship was scuttled, tubeworms have invaded much of the structure, and jewel anemones have begun to cluster on the upper surfaces. Leatherjackets and juvenile snapper have made the ship their home. This ship still looks essentially as it did above water. The guns and other military equipment have been removed, but telephones still hang from walls and the engines are still on board. Repeated dives are not only necessary to explore the ship, but they will be rewarded with the opportunity to watch the natural development of a new underwater habitat.

The *Canterbury*

Tidal forests

Stubby mangrove trees are common along most of Northland's coast. These saltwater forests provide an essential nursery and unique habitat for many species, and are also interesting places to snorkel. If there has been no rain for a week and the water is calm, head to the mangroves an hour or two before high tide. You won't be disappointed: schools of yellow-eyed and grey mullet glide through the water; flounder settle on the floor; crabs scurry about; and barnacles sweep the water for minute specks of food. Be careful when the tide turns, as the outgoing tide brings strong currents and murky water. The best mangroves estuaries to visit are Manapouri (north of Tutukaka) and Whangateau (on the way to Goat Island Bay).

Putahataha Island

Location	Bay of Islands
Access	Boat
Type of dive	Reef, cave
Level	Open water
Snorkel	Yes
Depth range	0–20 m
Current	Moderate; can be strong on spring tides
When to dive	Anytime; afternoon sun is ideal
Look for	Bigeyes, porcupine fish, schools of parore, stingrays

This island has an unusual boulder landscape – it is one of the few places
where the boulders are not covered in *Ecklonia* kelp. This is not to say
that the boulders are completely bare; like many of the rocks you find in
Northland, they are covered in colourful encrusting life. As you enter the
water, you are likely to encounter large schools of parore feeding at the
surface. At a depth of about 10 m, the west-facing entrance to a large cave
appears. The entranceway is fringed with colourful soft corals, anemones,
and sea urchins; and is home to pigfish, moray eels and hiwihiwi. Inside the
cave, light is reflected from the white sand bottom at 18 m, where short-
tailed stingrays often rest. The sculpted cave walls lead to an undulating
ceiling where thousands of bigeyes congregate. After leaving the cave, swim
over the shallow boulders and valleys: you'll encounter lots of sandagers
wrasse and many small hydroid trees.

The *Rainbow Warrior*

Location	Southwest of Motutapere Island, Cavalli Islands
Access	Boat
Type of dive	Wreck
Level	Advanced or experienced open water
Snorkel	No
Depth range	12–30 m
When to dive	Anytime
Current	Light, but can be strong on spring tides
Look for	Jewel anemones, John Dory, shipwreck

The *Rainbow Warrior* was the first of Northland's chain of recreational diving wrecks when she was sunk here in 1987. Two decades later, the ship has become a favourite of many divers, and a favoured reef for many animals. The rails are almost corroded away, a few holes have appeared

in the hull, and the wheel house lies broken on the sandy sea floor after succumbing to gravity. But every surface that remains is covered with a rich invertebrate carpet. Luminous pink jewel anemones were early colonisers of the ship, and many remain. The particularly colourful stern hull is an exquisite example of this. Elsewhere on the ship, other invertebrates and algae have muscled their way in as the reef ages. *The Rainbow Warrior* is lying on a slight angle, with the port deck sitting at about 18 m, the starboard deck about 21 m and the bow hovering above the 25–26 m sand sea floor. A dark and cavernous room near the bow is a favourite gathering place of usually cave-dwelling bigeyes. You'll find all kinds of fish around the wreck: large snapper, red mullet, John Dory, leatherjackets, and, especially in the summer months, schools of koheru.

Neptune's Garden

Neptune's Garden

Location	Between Tuturuowae and Nukutaunga islands, Cavalli Islands
Access	Boat
Type of dive	Reef, cave, sandy bottom, kelp
Level	Open water
Snorkel	Yes
Depth range	0–25 m
When to dive	Not in northwesterlies or northern swell
Current	None
Look for	Eagle rays, cave, sponges, crayfish

Neptune was the Roman god of the sea, and this lovely bay is an underwater garden fit for any god. Anchored in a boulder bay, the first animals you are likely to encounter are eagle rays, that is if they are not too upset by your arrival and hang around. Close by is the cave entrance at a depth of about 10 m. The entrance is an unusual shape – it is more of a vertical crack with a bulbous base. The crack extends to the sea surface, but narrows too snugly for divers to ascend. Outside of the cave is an enticing colourful maze of cracks and gutters. Many are wide enough (about 1–2 m) for divers to swim through. You'll find yourself in shallow canyons, where the walls on both sides are covered in vibrant invertebrate life. The top of these pinnacles and boulders are covered with a dense and varied seaweed garden. You'll find scorpion fish and crayfish among the cracks and boulders, their bright colours blending imperceptibly with their surroundings.

Neptune's Garden

Lord Howe coral fish

Unique in the marine world for having one mate for life, you'll encounter pairs of these fish fossicking around the reef with their long snouts. The first identified home of these striped fish was Lord Howe Island, a small Pacific island between Australia and New Zealand that boasts the southern-most coral reef in the world. The East Auckland Current flows past Northland, bringing warmer

northern Pacific water and a few stray tropical species with it. Some, such as the Lord Howe coral fish (*Amphichaetodon howensis*), have stayed and are now well established on northern reefs, especially at the Poor Knights Islands.

Twin Wrecks

Location	Tutukaka Coast
Access	Boat
Type of dive	Wreck
Level	Advanced
Snorkel	No
Depth range	20–34 m
When to dive	Calm sea conditions; the *Waikato* is best dived at high tide to avoid currents and the low visibility run-off at low tide
Current	The *Waikato* is subject to current and poor visibility with an out-going tide; current is slight on the *Tui*, but may be stronger in spring tides
Look for	Jewel anemones, John Dory, schools of porae

Towards the end of last century, two Royal New Zealand Navy vessels were being decommissioned, so a group of enthusiasts set about the task of having them sunk close to Tutukaka, the gateway to the Poor Knights, to create two artificial reefs for recreational diving. The ships were scuttled a few kilometres apart, near the Tutukaka Heads: the smaller *Tui* in 1999 and the *Waikato* in 2000. The ocean swells have tousled and broken both ships, creating 'true' shipwrecks that offer interesting dives.

The *Tui*, a 62-m oceanographic research vessel, was used first by the American and subsequently the New Zealand Navy, although she was never armed. She was commissioned in 1971; was involved with various research projects; was officially part of New Zealand's anti-nuclear protest fleet at Mururua Atoll; and now lies in 34 m of water. She is lying on her port side, having slipped down a rocky reef. The stern is completely separated from the rest of the ship and lies twisted and overturned a short distance away, with its rudder sitting unnaturally upright. The ship's hull is being taken over by clusters of deep pink jewel anemones and small orange soft corals. You'll find goatfish grazing on the upturned hull; schools of bigeyes, porae and golden snapper sheltering inside the broken end of the vessel; and solitary John Dory swimming past. It's possible to complete a quick circumnavigation of the exterior of the entire ship in a single dive. On the

Tui

way back to the surface, you will almost certainly want to include a safety stop on the jewel anemone encrusted buoy line. You'll probably be accompanied by clouds of sweep as you do so.

The *Waikato* is a 137-m frigate that is similar to the *Canterbury* scuttled in the Bay of Islands. However, when she was sunk, all of her guns were left intact, as was her propeller, and as such is the more complete shipwreck. The *Waikato* lies in shallower water than the *Tui* (about 30 m) but is simply too large to explore in a single dive. In fact, it would take several dives to really explore this wreck. Four individual buoy lines lead you to the bow, the guns, the wheelhouse or the stern. The bow, where the guns are attached, has broken away forward of the ship's wheelhouse and lies on its port side. Jewel and daisy anemones cover most surfaces. Leatherjackets are usually seen hovering above the ship.

A swim across the 10–15 m divide that separates the two ship halves, will take you to the wheelhouse and back of the ship. Much of the ship is penetrable, and the original ship's structure is easily understood. The ceiling of the wheelhouse has a lining of jewel anemones and, if you're lucky, you might find a kingfish or two inside.

Waikato

Tui

Waikato

Waikato

Tui

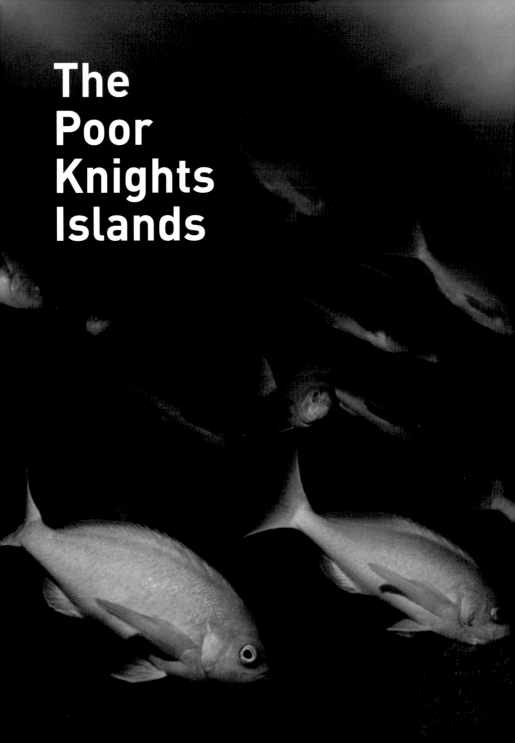

The
Poor
Knights
Islands

Red Baron Caves

Mention the Poor Knights to almost any New Zealand diver and you will likely be asked: 'Did you know that Jacques Cousteau once rated the Poor Knights as one of the top 10 diving locations in the world?' It is not so much

Middle Arch

a question as a statement of fact – an absolute truth among Kiwi diving enthusiasts. And who would argue? Certainly not the thousands of recreational divers who have visited the Poor Knights since France's most famous scuba diver.

This offshore island group lies a little over 20 km east of the small Northland port of Tutukaka – far enough offshore to benefit from clear oceanic blue water, yet close enough that a day trip from the

mainland is feasible. The water is teeming with life: vast schools of fish swim past colourful walls of anemones, sponges, bryozoans, algae and ascidians. As well as the anticipated temperate species, some sub-tropical animals are swept towards the islands by the East Auckland Current, culminating in a unique blend of temperate and sub-tropical underwater life. Some of the visitors, such as the Lord Howe coral fish and spotted black grouper, have relocated permanently. While others, for example turtles, just pass through from time to time.

Blue Maomao Arch

The Poor Knights Islands comprise the main island group (Tawhiti Rahi, Aorangi, Aorangaia and Archway islands), a group of pinnacles (The Pinnacles) 6 km to the south, and a single rock (Sugarloaf Rock) a further 2 km south. All offer spectacular diving, although the isolation and tiny above-water landmass of The Pinnacles and Sugarloaf Rock make access to them difficult at times.

The main island group was once inhabited by Maori but, under attack from another Northland tribe, they escaped to mainland New Zealand and the islands have been uninhabited by humans ever since.

The Poor Knights Islands were named by Captain James Cook, who first sighted them in 1760. It is widely believed the name came from an English pudding, popular on board Cook's ships. But other accounts describe Cook naming them the Poor Knights partly because they looked like reclining soldiers, and partly in deference to the Three Kings Islands further north, that Abel Tasman had named many years prior. Subsequently, The Pinnacles and Sugarloaf Rock were named the Poor Squires.

The Poor Knights, which remain rodent-free, have been in the hands of the New Zealand government since 1882 and, since 1975, the land flora and fauna have been completely protected. In turn, the islands have become a refuge for many unique New Zealand species, including tuatara, several lizard species and many scarce land invertebrates. The islands are also an important nesting ground for sea birds, with several petrel and shearwater species nesting here. So important is this natural habitat, people are prohibited from landing on the islands without special permission.

39

The ancient volcanic landscape is full of cracks, fissures and sheer cliffs. There are no beaches, and the water has eroded the porous rock into shapes that defy gravity. Cliff faces descend precipitously to the water's edge and continue to plummet beneath the waves – sheer vertical walls encrusted with life lead to a sandy sea floor 50 m below.

The underwater landscape is pitted with fissures, caves, arches and tunnels. Huge underwater caverns become a haven for shy animals, or a resting place out of the sun for schools of busy fish.

Ngaio Rock

Divers are attracted to the vast schools of fish – a shimmering of blue, pink and silver in clear blue water – that congregate in the many archways, as well as to the spectacular underwater scenery.

Ironically, it was a fisherman, not a diver, who first recognised the uniqueness of the Poor Knights Islands. American adventurer, Zane Grey, lauded the area's potential as a big-game fishing ground in the 1920s, cementing the destiny of the Poor Knights Islands as New Zealand's premier fishing location. In the following decades, many New Zealanders agreed. They flocked to the area to dive and spearfish, and were not disappointed by the large and diverse schools of fish.

Fortunately, the Poor Knights Islands became New Zealand's second marine reserve in 1981. Initially, recreational fishing and spearfishing were permitted, but fish numbers failed to fully recover. Finally, in 1998, the entire area, including The Pinnacles and Sugarloaf Rock became fully protected.

The Poor Knights Islands are home to dozens of dive sites, all of them submerged in clear blue water and inhabited by thousands of fish: you won't be disappointed by any of them. Access to many of the dive sites is restricted in certain weather or sea conditions, but you can always find a sheltered site somewhere at the Knights. It has been an onerous task to single out just a few, but we have selected six of the best that we think offer something unique from each other.

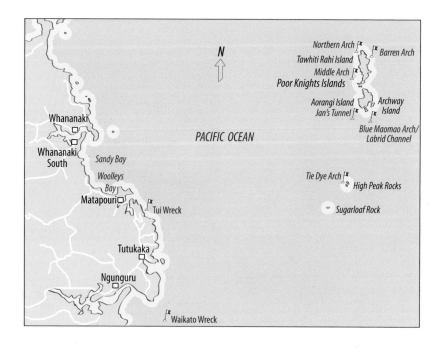

The Poor Knights Islands

Diving at
Poor Knights

The underwater visibility at the Knights is usually very good, but best from February to September, when it averages around 20 m. On some winter days, it might be in excess of 30 m. After September, the visibility begins to drop off, and is particularly affected by spring plankton blooms. But even in spring and early summer (October–January) visibility is rarely less than 10 m. As an added bonus, stingrays visit the archways in the summer months. The water temperature ranges from 15–16°C (59–60°F) May–September to 20–23°C (68–73°F) January–April.

Labrid Channel

Northern Arch
Marine Reserve

Location	Northwest Tawhiti Rahi Island
Access	Boat
Type of dive	Wall and archway
Level	Advanced
Snorkel	Yes
Depth range	0–45 m
When to dive	Slack water, easterly and westerly conditions; never in strong northerly conditions
Current	Strong tidal current at all depths; in westerly conditions, surface current may be strong
Look for	Stingrays, schools of golden snapper, blue maomao, demoiselles, golfball sponges, kingfish

If the Poor Knights are New Zealand's premier diving location, then this spectacular dive site is one the country's absolute best dive sites. It can be dived from either of the two bays that are connected by the archway, but the usually calm Maomao Bay on the northern side is a great place to start. As you view the small opening in the rock that is the apex of Northern Arch, the visible part of the archway gives no clues as to the depth and grandeur of the underwater shaft awaiting exploration: the walls lead straight down to the sea floor at 35–40 m. Looking down into the shaft, the narrowest point occurs around 12 m below the water where the walls are a mere 3–4 m apart; at its widest, the arch is more than 13 m wide. The slight undulations, indentations and underhangs provide wonderful places for creatures to take refuge from the current that is almost always present.

The Poor Knights Islands

Look for moray eels, nudibranchs, painted moki, gold ribbon grouper and Lord Howe coral fish among the colourful encrusted walls, where pink gorgonians and delicate bryozoans nudge each other in the dense invertebrate jungle. Although the walls are fascinating and provide an interesting safety stop, the schools of fish are the highlight of this dive. Out in the middle of the archway, you'll share the current with schools of golden snapper, blue and pink maomao and demoiselles, and, in the summer months, stingrays. As these graceful giants glide through and up and down the archway, they resemble fighter planes flying in stacked formation, and create an eerie atmosphere that has been likened to Gotham City, the home of Batman.

Northern Arch's boulder bottom is covered in colourful yellow and orange golf ball sponges, and schools of porae and golden snapper are often seen hovering above the sponge gardens. This is a spectacular and dramatic dive site, but is subject to current, and it is easy to descend deeper and stay longer than you intend. Watch the current and your depth – the water clarity and sheer walls sometimes make even the most seasoned diver giddy. You can take refuge and complete your dive by slowly meandering up the wall. A shallow cruise or snorkel around the encrusted rocky edge of the bay makes a great finish to a dive here.

Northern Arch

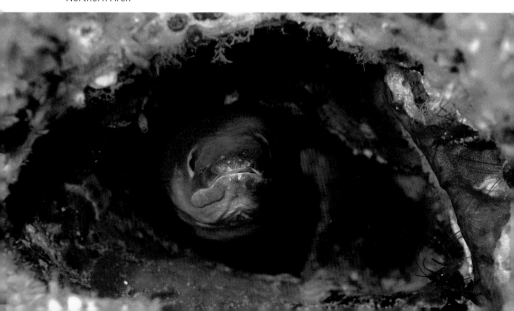

Barren Arch
Marine Reserve

Location	Northeast Tawhiti Rahi Island
Access	Boat
Type of dive	Wall and archway
Level	Open water
Snorkel	Yes
Depth range	6–35 m
When to dive	Westerly condition; no easterly swells
Current	None, but the northern entrance is subject to surge
Look for	Schools of pink and blue maomao, mado, demoiselles, colourful sponges and invertebrate life

This underwater connection between two bays has abundant sea life, in contrast to its name, which was allegedly bestowed upon it in order to deter spearfishermen from visiting in the days when the Poor Knights was not a marine reserve. Whether this is folklore, or the archway was indeed barren, it certainly could never be described as such today: this magnificent archway is now home to hundreds of fish. You can approach the dive site from either the northern of southern bay, and the archway – through which a small boat can pass – is visible above water. The northern end of the archway is the shallowest (around 6–7 m) and you have to glide over an even shallower (2–3 m) kelp covered ridge to enter this way, which is relatively easy but subject to surge.

Underwater, the archway slopes down to a maximum depth of 35 m at the southern end; in the middle is a cavernous space that is often filled with large schools of blue and pink maomao. They frequently cluster around a 6-m deep rocky ledge – reminiscent of a theatre balcony – on the eastern wall. The sea floor is covered with large boulders, and the walls that lead to the boulder bottom are covered in colourful sponges, bryozoans and anemones. Closer inspection walls reveals a rainbow of life: moray eels, nudibranchs and invertebrates make their home among colourful jewel anemones, sponges and bryozoans. Close to the floor you may encounter a large school of mado fish – the largest you are ever likely to see.

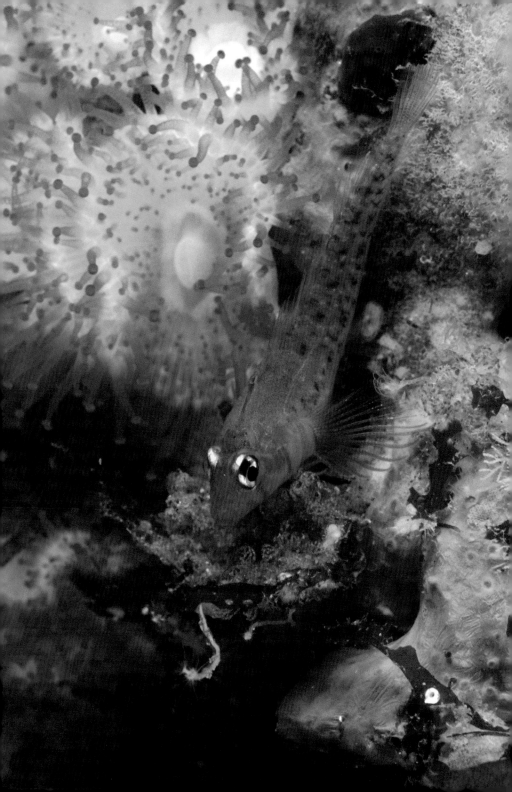

Rikoriko Cave

The largest sea cave in the world?

Rikoriko cave is the largest sea cave in New Zealand, and thought to be the largest volume sea cave in the world. Rikoriko, meaning the cave of sounds or dancing light, is a blister cave, the remnant of a large gas bubble formed during a volcanic eruption thousands of years ago. Erosion has revealed the 12 m-high entrance that gives little clue as to the huge auditorium-sized cavern within. The acoustics of the cave have enticed many visitors to test their voice, and many musicians have performed in the dark acoustic chamber.

Length 130 m

Width 80 m

Inside height above sea 35 m

Underwater depth 26 m

Inside surface area 1 ha

Total volume over 220,000 m³

Middle Arch and Bernie's Cave
Marine Reserve

Location	West Tawhiti Rahi Island
Access	Boat
Type of dive	Wall and cave
Level	Open water
Snorkel	Yes
Depth range	0–40 m
When to dive	Northerly and southeasterly conditions
Current	Light to moderate in archway
Look for	Mosaic moray eels, Spanish lobsters, nudibranchs, *Diadema palmeri*

The 12 m-high rocky surround of Middle Arch is easy to spot once anchored in the sheltered southeast bay. As with many of the archways at the Knights, the walls plummet steeply underwater. The boulder bottom is home to moray eels – brush aside the *Ecklonia* kelp to find the yellow, grey and mosaic moray eels that wind themselves in between the boulders.

As you ascend the walls, look closely for nudibranchs, cleaner wrasse

stations and crested blennies among the dense invertebrate garden. Bright yellow zoanthids, delicate jewel anemones and encrusting sponges in yellow, orange and red cover almost every surface. Jostling for space are ascidians, bryozoans, hydroids and gorgonians. In the blue water of the centre of the archway, look for schools of blue and pink maomao, demoiselles and leatherjackets.

On the southwestern wall of the archway, at about 6 m deep, you will find the entrance to Bernie's Air Bubble Cave. In this large cave – with a small air cavity in its roof – schools of demoiselles and scorpion fish lie in wait on the sandy bottom. Shining a torch onto the cave walls will reveal more colourful invertebrate life and an occasional firebrick star, moray eel or *Diadema palmeri*. Look for Lord Howe coral fish, pipefish among the kelp, and black spotted grouper – all have been spotted here.

The Poor Knights Islands

Jan's Tunnel

Jan's Tunnel

Jan's Tunnel

Jan's Tunnel
Marine Reserve

Location	Southwest Aorangi Island
Access	Boat
Type of dive	Wall and boulder bottom
Level	Open water and advanced
Snorkel	Yes
Depth range	0–55 m
When to dive	Northerly and easterly conditions, no swell, night
Current	Slight
Look for	*Diadema palmeri*, nudibranchs, scarlet wrasse, warratah anemones

Jan's Tunnel should have something to satisfy almost every diver. This is really two dives in one: the first is an easy swim through a long channel; the second a fairly deep dive to a sponge and gorgonian garden. If you swim about 45 m along the narrow channel leading inland, you eventually arrive at another equally narrow tunnel. Swim a further 14 m inland and you will find yourself in a small lagoon about 16 m across. Along the channel and lagoon walls, there are hundreds of blood-red warratah anemones clinging to the rock walls, just below the tide line. A little deeper are the cup corals. The channel walls, pockmarked with small holes, are ideal habitats for all kinds of interesting invertebrate life, as well as small fish. There are a few caves and holes to the left of the lagoon entrance, which should be  entered only by experienced cave divers. When you swim back out of the channel, explore the area to the south of the channel entrance, where there are some more tunnels and caves to explore.

For a deep-water dive, swim past a group of submerged pinnacles, then descend about 10–15 m. Swim out to sea until the sea floor becomes visible before descending to 40–50 m. There you will find a fairyland of large yellow finger sponges and pink gorgonian fans, with butterfly perch, long-fin boarfish and scarlet wrasse hovering close by.

Blue Maomao Arch and Labrid Channel
Marine Reserve

Location	Aorangi Island, northeast of Archway Island
Access	Boat
Type of dive	Wide and open cave
Level	Open water
Snorkel	Yes
Depth range	0–15 m
When to dive	Northerly or southerly conditions, calm conditions, afternoon in full sun
Current	Can be strong in channel
Look for	Schools of blue maomao, long-finned boarfish, many different fish

The top of the arch is visible above water and large enough to drive a small boat through, but the dive itself is more like a tunnel, which is about 40 m long. In the middle of this tunnel is an overhead opening through which afternoon sun pours into the otherwise dark tunnel, producing an ethereal blue curtain of light. In the winter months, when the sun is lower in the sky, these dramatic shafts of light extend across the width of the archway. Through this stunning underwater light show, schools of blue maomao, the fish who lend their name to the dive site, swim past. They shelter inside the tunnel, drifting in large masses with the water movement. But these are not the only fish to be found here: schools of demoiselles, sandager wrasse, mado, trevally and pigfish also frequent this dive site. And occasionally, a spotted black grouper has been seen. The walls of the tunnel are covered in bryozoans. Look for nudibranchs and moray eels, especially the speckled variety.

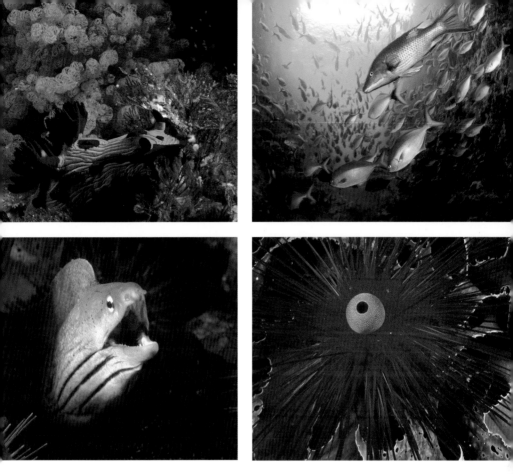

You enter Blue Maomao Arch from Labrid Channel, and rather than just being the conduit to a great dive site, Labrid Channel itself merits some exploration. The sandy sea floor is scattered with kelp-covered boulders and lots of different species of fish swim through the shallow channel. Look for stingrays, wrasses, scorpion fish, moray eels and hat urchins buried in the sand. The southern wall of Aorangi Island is a great place to find smaller fish and invertebrates nestled on the steep walls.

Ngaio Rock, truly not more than a small rock visible above water at the western aspect of Labrid Channel, is another very worthy dive site. Underwater, its steep walls descend to 25 m and are crammed with marine life. Dense *Ecklonia* kelp colonies give way to purple gorgonians and bryozoans in brilliant yellow and red. Many invertebrates cling to the wall, including the gorgeous blue and yellow *Tambja verconis* nudibranch and the striking red sea urchin, *Diadema palmeri*.

Blue Maomao Arch

Maomao relations?

Two fish you will definitely encounter at Poor Knights Islands are blue and pink maomao. They congregate in large schools in archways, cave entrances, around pinnacles and in the mid-blue water. Both are plankton feeders and swim around in schools, but there the similarity ends. They are, in fact, not related to each other. Pink maomao are members of the grouper family and tend to gather in mid water. Blue maomao are a type of stonebream and usually hover closer to the water surface. Both take their common name from the Maori name for the blue fish: maomao; pink maomao are known as matata in Maori.

Tie Dye Arch
Marine Reserve

Location	The Pinnacles
Access	Boat
Type of dive	Wall and archway
Level	Open water
Snorkel	No
Depth range	0–25 m
When to dive	In calm conditions with little or no swell
Current	Moderate; strong at times
Look for	Colourful invertebrate life, porae, golden snapper, stingrays in summer, moray eels

If you are old enough to remember the sixties and seventies, cast your mind back to the psychedelic phenomenon of tie-dyed clothing. Remember the erratic uncertainty of the outcome? Just the sure knowledge that the effect would be startling, colourful and unpredictable. These three adjectives aptly describe one of the Poor Knights best dive sites. The exposed and craggy pinnacles give little clue to the huge underwater cave and archway that lies beneath the water surface. Although this is reminiscent of other archways found in the Knights, it just seems larger. And even more colourful. The walls are covered with encrusting sponges in every shade of yellow and orange. Anemones, bryozoans, zoanthids, hydroids and sponges cluster side by side. Look closely and you will find many different nudibranchs and moray eels living on these colourful walls.

Boats usually anchor to the southwest of the largest pinnacle, from where it's a short swim down to the southwest entrance about 3 m underwater. Keep swimming and the vast archway becomes apparent at about 10 m. Swim through this

and you will find yourself inside the cave-like archway itself. There are three different entrances into the huge submerged cavern. For a truly spectacular dive, descend to the bottom (about 20 m) and take a few moments to view the towering archway above. You'll be butting up against the largest, most gloriously coloured boulders you will see at the Knights. Some are as big as cars, and they are all densely colonised by brightly coloured encrusting sponges. It is likely you will have the company of a school of golden snapper and porae hovering in the blue gloom. As you slowly ascend alongside breathtaking archway walls, you'll be sharing the water with schools of blue maomao, trevally and, in summer months, short-tailed stingrays.

This dive site is particularly exposed to sea conditions. As a result, it is a real treat to be able to get in the water here. Perhaps the infrequency of visitors allows the fish to congregate freely and undisturbed. This dive rarely disappoints.

The Hauraki Gulf

Burgess Island, Mokohinau Islands

Mokohinau Islands

The Hauraki Gulf was once a low-lying plain. It was flooded after the meltdown of the last ice age – approximately 12,000 years ago – and has remained underwater ever since. The gulf's coastline is more than 2000 km long and takes many forms: rocky shores abut steep cliff faces; flax covered banks lead to gently sloping sandy beaches; stubby mangrove trees emerge from flat and muddy estuaries. This unique marine area forms the Hauraki Gulf Marine Park, established in 2000 to protect the area adjacent to New Zealand's largest city.

On the eastern side, the Coromandel Peninsula extends like a long finger to enclose a shallow horseshoe-shaped bay. The Firth of Thames is an important marine bird sanctuary and marks the southern boundary of the gulf. The northeastern boundary is loosely identified by a chain of scattered islands that includes: the Hen and Chickens, a group of islands that is said to resemble a mother hen (Taranga Island) leading her five chicks (Marotiri Islands) behind, and are an important tuatara habitat; the Mokohinau Islands, which offer diverse underwater habitats and marine animals, including bigger species such as marlin, shark, kingfish and hapuku; Little Barrier Island (Hauturu), with near original (unchanged by man or animals) native forest, where many land species live, as well as such sea birds as blue penguins, terns, gannets, petrels and shearwaters; and Great Barrier Island (Aotea), one of the largest and most diverse islands in the gulf.

Snapper

These carnivorous fish are one of the most commonly sighted and caught of the gulf's species. Snapper (*Pagrus auratus*) are found all around New Zealand, but are more common north of Cook Strait. They are all female when born and about half will undergo a sex-change at 3–4 years old. An adult snapper has no trouble smashing the hard shells of its favourite foods – sea urchins, crabs and paua – and will eventually grow to over one metre long and more than 50 years old, if allowed.

The Hauraki Gulf

Aotea has been the subject of extensive marine research. On its northern coast, scientists have discovered over 60 different species of seaweed, including southern bull kelp that is normally found further south. More than 70 different fishes can be seen here, including more blennies and triplefins that you will ever find on the mainland. These are just a few of the 50 or so islands contained within the Hauraki Gulf. Many are the remnants of volcanic activity; others are relatively intact but extinct volcanoes. Some, like Hauturu, erupted millions of years ago, while others such as Rangitoto, erupted just 600 years ago.

The Hauraki Gulf is also home to New Zealand's most famous and most accessible marine reserve – The Cape Rodney-Okakari Point Marine Reserve, or Goat Island Bay - which was established in 1975. In the 32 years since fish numbers in the reserve have increased dramatically. The University of Auckland established a marine laboratory overlooking Goat Island Bay in 1962, so the study of marine life here has been extensive both before and after the launch of the marine reserve.

Goat Island Bay

Mokohinau Islands

Mokohinau Islands

The Hauraki Gulf

Before the reserve was established, the underwater environment had been stripped of many fish. Kina (sea urchins) had prospered in a predator-reduced environment that was full of their favourite food: kelp. Subsequently, the kina decimated the kelp beds. The result was a barren underwater landscape, rich in kina, but little else. After the reserve was established and fishing prohibited, fish life flourished. The fish feasted on the prolific kina and the kelp started to grow again. Finally, balance was restored, and the bay now teems with all kinds of marine life. Blue cod are three times more common inside the reserve than the surrounding waters, while snapper are 16 times more common. Not only are fish more common, they are bigger. Don't be surprised to see a 10-kg snapper.

The Hauraki Gulf, with its diverse coastline and close offshore islands, offers some of the most accessible diving and snorkelling in New Zealand. Diving here is as varied as the coastline: many of the gulf's most dramatic dive sites are located on or around volcanic islands or rock formations. The islands offer fantastic deep-water drop-offs to explore and plenty of easy coastal snorkelling, while the mangrove estuaries offer unique shallow-water experiences. Coastal access is relatively easy, and there are many organised boat trips to the islands.

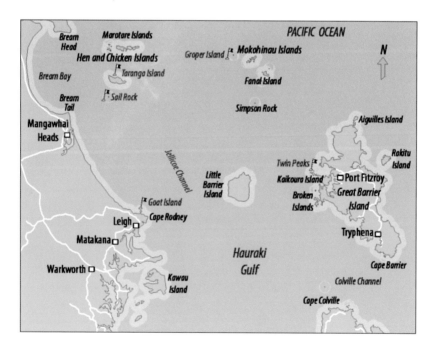

The Hauraki Gulf

Diving in the Hauraki Gulf

You can snorkel or dive along the coast or near many of the Hauraki Gulf islands, or take charter boats to the offshore island groups. Underwater visibility varies greatly, depending on where you dive. Expect 8–15 m in summer, and 10-20 m in winter ,with clearer water as you head further offshore. The visibility tends to be better in winter, but more fishy during the summer months, especially January and February. The outer Gulf islands benefit from the warm East Auckland Current that sweeps through the area. Water temperature ranges from 15–16°C (59-60°F) during May to September, to 20–23°C (68–73°F) during January to April.

Mokohinau Islands

Goat Island Bay
Marine Reserve

Location	Leigh
Access	Shore
Type of dive	Sandy bottom with kelp and rocks
Level	Open water
Snorkel	Yes
Depth range	0–20 m
When to dive	High tide; almost all conditions, except northerly or strong easterly conditions
Current	Minimal; watch the channel when the tide is running
Look for	Snapper, blue maomao, moki, stingrays

An estimated 250,000 people visit Goat Island Bay each year. This very sheltered bay is the perfect spot for novice divers and snorkellers. It's not a deep dive; the water isn't crystal clear; and you won't find shipwrecks or caves to explore, nor any fantastic coral formations. But you will encounter fish – lots and lots of fish.

Entering the water from the beach, the rocky shoreline on the right may be submerged or dry, depending on the tide. You will almost immediately encounter inquisitive fish, among them will certainly be a snapper or two. Previous feeding, now banned, has resulted in a resident school of snapper that are more inquisitive than the average fish. Don't feed them: it makes them quite aggressive. Instead, marvel at the coppery sheen of New Zealand's most recognisable fish.

As you swim further from the shore, occasional kelp-covered boulders appear on the gently sloping sandy sea floor. There is a channel between the mainland and Goat Island itself, where schools of snapper congregate. The eastern edge of the channel, which slopes gently down to a sand bottom at a depth of about 15-20 m, is the

home of eagle rays and stingrays. Be wary of currents, especially at the change of tide. Look under the kelp – there are certain to be many shells and crustaceans, small eggs and fish. Look into rocky holes and crevasses for bigeyes and on the rocks for hiwihiwi, triplefins. Look for parore and butterfish grazing on the kelp, and for blue cod, red goatfish and porae fossicking on the sandy sea floor. Watch as schools of blue maomao, demoiselles, silver drummers and individual moki, trevally, paketi and kahawai swim past. You will encounter many of New Zealand's coastal fish here.

If you're feeling adventurous, you can swim out to the island, about 140 m offshore, or around it if you are able and have the time. It's a 3-km trip around the island. In the deeper waters around the northern edge of Goat Island, you will find a nice sponge garden. For experienced divers and snorkellers, there are a number of small caves on the southeastern side of the island, and two large sea caves on the northern, or open ocean side of the island. Alternatively, one of the local boat operators can take you there. Goat Island Bay is also a great place to go night diving.

The Hauraki Gulf

Goat Island Bay

Goat Island Bay

Sail Rock

Location	Hen and Chicken Islands
Access	Boat
Type of dive	Reef and kelp
Level	Open water and advanced (north and western faces)
Snorkel	Yes
Depth range	0–40 m
When to dive	Anytime
Current	None
Look for	Kingfish, crayfish and, in summer, stingrays

This massive rock soars 138 m above the sea surface about 3.7 km south of Taranga or Hen Island, the largest island in the Hen and Chicken Islands. This is an interesting underwater landscape. Strap weed sways above a seemingly bare rocky platform with a smattering of daisy anemones at around 10 m deep. Descending further – between 10 and 30 m – huge boulders, some as big as vans, sit on top of one another, creating a maze of tunnels and caverns that are topped with *Ecklonia* kelp. This intricate array is the habitat and hideout of red moki, marblefish and crayfish, while schools of kingfish and snapper swim nearby. A large cave on the northeastern side of the rock, at about 10 m deep, is a favourite hiding place for bigeyes. Look for rock cod and crayfish as well. The shallower waters are frequented by schools of blue maomao, demoiselles and parore, which feed near the water surface, and large schools of energetic koheru zooming about, in focused feeding mode, at the water surface. In the shallows (2–5 m), you find some very interesting rock formations. Scattered throughout the rock are holes that resemble bomb craters. Some are almost perfectly round vertical holes, occasionally reaching over one metre deep, that look as if they have been drilled.

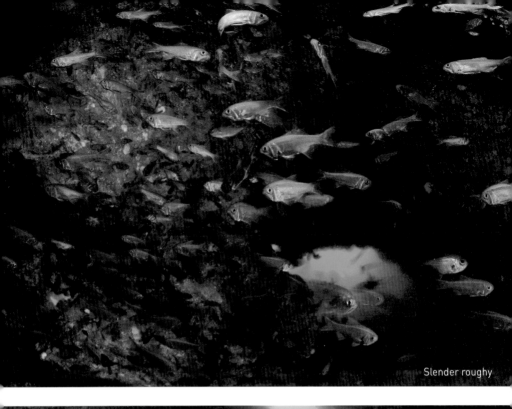
Slender roughy

Taranga Island (Hen Island)

Location	Hen and Chicken Islands
Access	Boat
Type of dive	Reef
Level	Open water
Snorkel	Yes
Depth range	0–30 m
When to dive	Winter for visibility
Current	None
Look for	Porcupine fish, crayfish and, in summer, stingrays

The mother, Hen Island, the largest in the group, stands 416 m above sea-level. The entire northern side of the island is worthy of exploration, though it will take several dives to take it all in. As you first descend into the water, the landscape is barren. You'll find yourself hovering above a large field of white boulders. Kelp is strangely absent, with just some straggly *Ecklonia* kelp clinging to the tops of the larger boulders. The tumbled boulder slope is a fish-sized maze of gaps, holes and tunnels. You'll easily find red moki, goatfish, marblefish, crayfish, and even porcupine fish in this open landscape.

Some of the large boulders form caverns that are large enough to crawl into: look for purple-grey finger sponges, anemones and crayfish inside. Silver drummers, leatherjackets, and a few demoiselles enjoy the wide open spaces, as do stingrays in summer months.

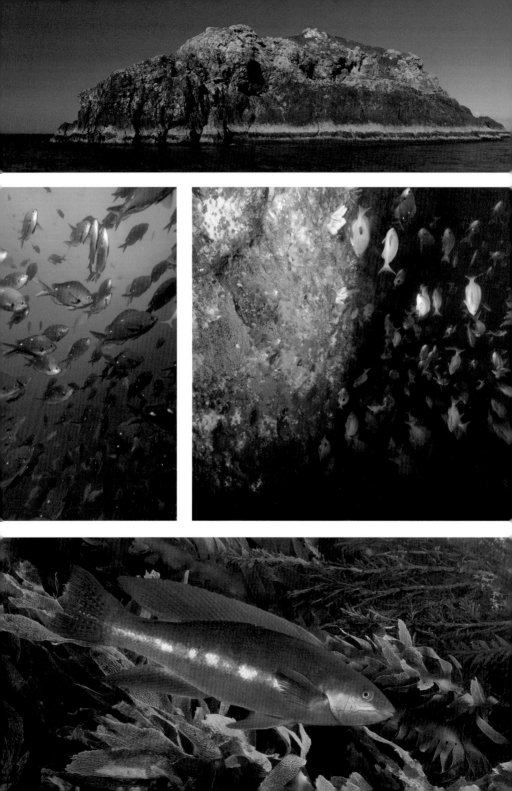

Tatapihi Island (Groper Island)

Location	Mokohinau Islands
Access	Boat
Type of dive	Wall
Level	Open water on south side; advanced on north side
Snorkel	Yes
Depth range	0–60 m
When to dive	Winter for visibility
Current	Light
Look for	Kingfish, pink maomao, butterfish and, in summer, stingrays and manta rays

Groper Island rises from 100-m deep-blue water. You will be taken aback by two things when you first get into the water on the northern side of the island: the vast numbers of fish and the inky blue depths into which the vertical wall drops away. Soon, at a depth of about 10 m, demoiselles will swarm all around you, while large pink maomao will be hovering beneath you. The fish are so dense that you may not be able to see the vibrant wall beside you. Swimming south, with the wall to your right, you'll pass vivid encrusting sponges, jewel anemones, and orange soft corals and other sponges. Pink maomao will swarm past, always repositioning themselves beside or below divers. You'll come to a small round cave (about 15 m deep) that at 4 m across is just big enough to swim easily in and out of. The inside of the cave offers another invertebrate assortment, but with the unusual addition of brachiopods. The demoiselles that huddle in the entrance will move out of your way.

As you travel further along the wall, you'll encounter plenty of fish: butterfish, red moki, marblefish, silver drummers, black angel fish, scorpion fish and moray eels – they simply have few places to hide as the wall is covered in very short kelp. At the south end of the island and towards the end of the dive, at a depth of 4–5 m, you'll find a large kelp-covered shelf that leads to another cave.

Watch your depth and buoyancy on this mesmerising but potentially dangerous dive site.

Kelly Tarlton is widely regarded as the father of modern scuba diving in New Zealand. He was a treasure-hunter and world-renowned marine archaeologist whose life ended prematurely in 1985. With a team of divers, that included another diving pioneer, Wade Doak, he salvaged bullion from the wreck of the *Elingamite*, near the Three Kings Islands, and from many other ships, including the Rothschild jewels from the wreck of the *Tasmania* near Mahia on the East Coast. But he was also a visionary, an inventor, a leader and entrepreneur. The proceeds of his treasure-hunting were used to build his ultimate dream – a world-first, walk-through underwater aquarium giving landlubbers the opportunity to experience some of the magic of the underwater world he loved. And divers love it, too. Auckland, home of Kelly Tarlton's Underwater World, is also the gateway to the Hauraki Gulf.

Twin Peaks

Location	Northern entrance to Port Fitzroy, Great Barrier Island
Access	Boat
Type of dive	Pinnacle, rocky reef
Level	Experienced open water
Snorkel	No
Depth range	5–35 m
When to dive	Incoming tide; slack water
Current	Light with incoming tide, but strong with outgoing
Look for	Golden snapper, porae, finger sponges

Perfectly poised to take advantage of the passing currents these pinnacles, dubbed Twin Peaks, are a great example of Hauraki Gulf diving at its best. Aotea/Great Barrier Island has an extraordinarily diverse marine biomass, and these underwater peaks that rise from the sea floor about 300–400 m to the north of Motuhaku Island on Aotea's western coast offer a glimpse of this. The flat top of the main pinnacle reaches up to within 5 m of the water surface, yet the northeastern edge of the pinnacles almost completely disappears before your eyes.

Imagine the conical shape of an ice-cream cone and you will have a reasonably good mental picture of this dive site. Of course, the apex is not nearly as small, that would be geologically impossible, but the wider crown creates an interesting underwater environment. Beneath it are ledges, overhangs and archways full of fish.

After descending, swim with the rock on your right and, at a depth of 18–20 m, you will come across a large underwater archway. The nearly 10-m wide arch is the home territory of porae and golden snapper, along with large schools of bigeyes, butterfly perch, demoiselles and busy mado fish.

The pinnacles are covered in prolific invertebrate life, and this arch is no exception, the inner walls and ceiling coated with sponges, soft corals and anemones.

Outside the arch, invertebrate life is even more astonishing. Here, red mullet fish, banded wrasses, spotties and scarlet wrasses forage and rest among a vivid sponge garden full of finger and golf ball sponges, and orange soft corals. Out in the blue, large schools of sweep, demoiselles, snapper, silver drummer and kingfish swim by. In mid-summer, look for schools of giant boarfish in the sand gutters at around 25 m deep.

The Hauraki Gulf

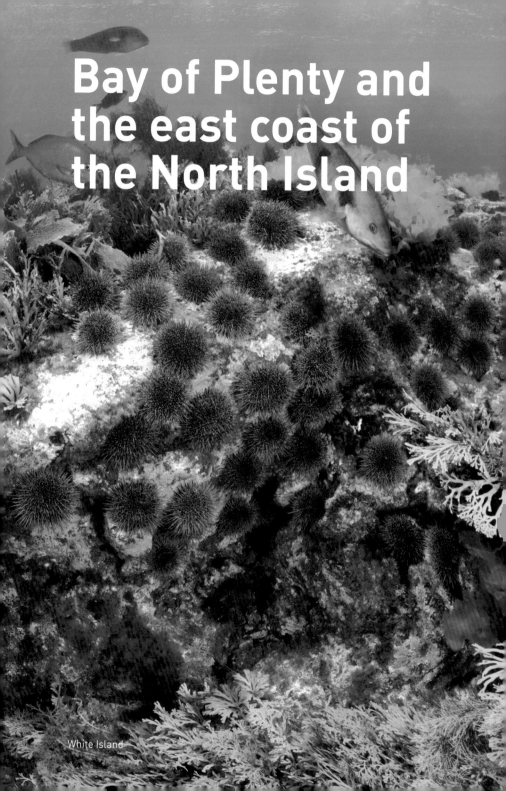

Bay of Plenty and the east coast of the North Island

White Island

The Coromandel Peninsula marks the start of the long eastern coastline of the North Island, a coastline that offers unique blue-water diving on the edge of the Pacific Ocean. The most eastern edge of the Bay of Plenty juts even further into the deep Pacific Ocean, and is the first part of mainland New Zealand to see the sun each day. It was also the first part of New Zealand to be sighted by Captain James Cook and the crew of the *Endeavour* on their trip to New Zealand in 1769.

There are few offshore islands along this coast and, as a result, those that do rise up from the sea floor are magnets for underwater life. The Alderman Islands, or Te Paepae Aotea, are an exquisite example of volcanic sculpture. From a distance, they look like any offshore island group – a few dark bumps on the horizon. But as you get closer, the bizarre formations that make up this odd collection of rocky pinnacles, needles and islands are matchless in any modern sculpture. At some point in the past, volcanic activity – one mighty blast, or perhaps many – has left craters, columns and rock chimneys over an area of 134 ha. These extraordinary shapes are a timely reminder of just how forceful volcanic eruptions can be. Beneath the waves, more columns reach, but don't quite make, the sea surface. This is a complex underwater environment, attracting both fish and humans.

Further down the coast, about 50 km northeast of Whakatane, is the island known to Maori as Whakaari, which James Cook named White

Island in reference to its perpetual appearance. New Zealand's only active marine volcano marks the tip of the volcanic belt that transects the North Island, and includes Rotorua, Taupo and Tongariro National Park.

Above water, White Island is barren – few plants and animals can survive in the harsh environment. Underwater, the environment couldn't be any more different. Rising from a very deep sea floor, the submerged volcano (most of its rocky mass) has become a magnet for oceanic fish and creatures.

The complex rocky landscape formed through previous volcanic explosions provides infinite places in which marine creatures can inhabit and hide. Every surface is covered in invertebrate life. Connected to White Island are the Volkner Rocks, a series of pinnacles that soar over 100 m into the sky from a submarine ridge 200 m below sea-level. Another pristine and abundant underwater habitat.

Champagne Bay, on the eastern side of White Island, is different again. Here, the surface of the water is covered with tiny bubbles, and underwater you'll find white holes with a chalky white rim. These volcanic vents release gas and warm water into the bay. The chalky white substance that covers the vent, and the fish that live inside it, is composed of anaerobic bacteria that survive on the sulphur released from the centre of the earth.

As Captain Cook travelled costal New Zealand, the names he bestowed on islands, bays and rocky headlands were all related to his state of mind at the time; his experience; or in honour of his crew or the English supporters of his voyages. So it was that the small bay where they first landed became known as The Bay of Poverty. Is it little wonder that local Maori were not keen to provide food to a crew who mistook their welcome as a challenge, and subsequently killed several of the welcoming party? Sailing further north, the *Endeavour* crew happened upon another bay, The Bay of Plenty, where local Maori were more welcoming, and food was plentiful. Underwater, the Bay of Plenty lives up to its name – plenty of life, plenty of visibility and plenty of dive locations. All along this long coastline, there are places you can drop into the water. Underwater, this area is a coast of plenty.

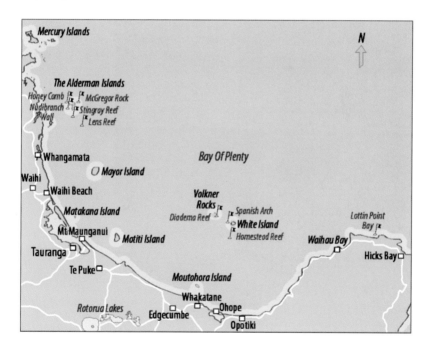

Bay of Plenty and the east coast of the North Island

Diving along the east coast of the North Island

You can snorkel or shore dive from much of the east coast of the North Island, or take charter boats to the offshore island groups. Underwater visibility throughout the area will vary greatly, depending on where you dive. Expect 8–20 m, with clearer water as you head further offshore. The visibility is not so dependent on water temperature, and the waters are more fishy during the summer months, especially January to March. The east coast benefits from the warm East Auckland Current that sweeps through the area. Water temperature ranges from 15–16°C (59–60°F) during May to September, to 20–23°C (68–73°F) from January to April.

Lottin Point Bay

Honeycomb

Location	Hongiora Island, Alderman Islands
Access	Boat
Type of dive	Cave, pinnacle
Level	Open water
Snorkel	Yes
Depth range	0–25 m
When to dive	Best in calm conditions with the afternoon sun to fill caverns with light
Current	Slight, but subject to surge
Look for	Caves, tunnels, bigeyes, crayfish, *Diadema palmeri*

This is a great cave dive for almost any diver, even those who feel a little nervous about being in enclosed spaces underwater. The rock formation is truly a honeycomb, a giant collection of caves and wide connecting corridors. Most of the system is open to the air and can be navigated by kayak. The bottom of the system is about 9 m, although outside of the entrances is around 15 m deep. You can swim over boulders to enter the system underwater, or simply drop down into one of the caves near the above-water opening.

There are three main caves that have football-sized boulders on the bottom, and are filled with bigeyes that scatter with approaching divers. As you look at the island, the first cave, to the left, is not visible above water, so it is likely you will enter the system via the next larger cave. At the back of this cavernous space is a large rock that is transformed into an orange and yellow blaze under torchlight. Yes, you will definitely need a torch to enjoy this dive. To your right will be the blue glow of a square passageway. It is a marvel of natural forces – the walls look like they have been sliced with a fine-bladed knife. The brightening blue light draws you along this passage and into another cave. From the back of this cave, two blue windows can be seen that lead though two archways into the fourth and final cave. From here, you can swim out into the open and explore the pinnacle in front of the second cave, where *Diadema palmeri* sea urchins cling to the sides. All through the cave system, you will be accompanied by bigeyes, while the sound of your breathing will be accompanied by rhythmic clangs and swishing sounds.

Young Nick's Head

One can only imagine the state of mind of a group of men who have been travelling for many months in an eighteenth century sailing ship. The pressing need to sight land and make landfall must surely have been unbearable.

On 24 September 1769, the crew of the *Endeavour* noticed seaweed floating in the water and Captain Cook, believing this a sure sign of land, promised a gallon of rum to any man who discovered the land. He then raised the stakes – two gallons of rum if it was spotted by nightfall.

Nicholas Young, a 12-year-old assistant to the ship's surgeon spotted the land while up one of the masts nearly two weeks later. The southern headland of Poverty Bay was named in his honour.

Known to Maori as Te Kuri A Paoa, the headland is believed to be the landing place of Maori canoes (waka) in 1350. One of the waka, *Horouta*, was captained by Paoa, and the landing site is named after his dog.

Nudibranch Wall

Location	Hongiora Island, Alderman Islands
Access	Boat
Type of dive	Wall
Level	Open water
Snorkel	Yes
Depth range	0–25 m
When to dive	All weather
Current	Slight to moderate
Look for	Nudibranchs, zoanthids and anemones

To some people they are butterflies of the sea; to others, sea slugs. However you describe these delightful little molluscs, they never fail to delight when you find them slowly meandering across a reef with their gills waving in

the water. As you might anticipate from the name of this dive site, this is a wall that is full of many different types of nudibranchs.

This dive starts on the southwestern side of Hongiora Island, just around from the Honeycomb, in a small bay near a hole that transects the island. With the wall on your left, swim around a point where the near vertical wall drops to the sand bottom at 25 m deep. The top 8 m of the wall are smothered in *Ecklonia* kelp, but sweeping that aside, you'll find sponges, bryozoans, yellow zoanthids, orange soft corals and anemones in a collage of colour and texture; and, of course, nudibranchs. As well as the nudibranchs, look for triplefins and moray eels. Do look out from the wall occasionally, as this dive can also be quite fishy: expect to see butterfly perch, blue and red moki, banded perch and stingrays. In the sand near the southwest corner of the wall, you can usually find sand eels at around 22–24 m deep.

Alderman Pinnacles

Location	Alderman Islands		
Access	Boat		
	McGregor's Rock	*Stingray Reef*	*Len's Reef*
Type of dive	Pinnacle	Pinnacle	Pinnacle
Level	Experienced open water	Open water	Advanced
Snorkel	No	No	No
Depth range	0–50 m	8–35 m	8–70 m
When to dive	Calm conditions no wind	Calm conditions	Calm and
Current	Strong currents currents	Moderate	Strong
Look for	Schooling fish, crayfish, kingfish, sharks, stingrays, eagle rays, moray eels		

The pinnacles that belong to the Alderman Island group offer some fantastic diving. You can't really imagine the underwater geology, let alone the marine life that is attracted to these pinnacles. Each pinnacle offers dramatically different diving and, since there are different locations, you should always be able to dive on one of them no matter what the conditions.

McGregor's Rock

This large rock, about one kilometre northeast of George Island, is neither an island nor completely submerged. At most, it stands one metre out of the water, but is constantly awash with the ocean swells. The rock's steep underwater walls plunge to 30 m, except at the southeastern aspect, which plummets to 50 m before sloping off. The brilliantly coloured vertical walls of this rock are neither flat, nor even, with overhangs and deep cracks providing safe havens for crayfish to shuffle backwards away from would-be human predators! The walls display the usual invertebrate mosaic, but look for nudibranchs, sponges and hydroids.

Almost from the moment you enter the water here, you'll be surrounded by fish: butterfish, red moki, leatherjackets, black angel fish and schools of koheru; large schools of blue maomao, with kawhai on the edge; and the occasional kingfish zooming through. Schools of butterfly perch hover in the deeper waters and weave around the top of the pinnacle. There can be strong currents and equally strong surges here, which makes for exciting diving but best for experienced divers. If that isn't exciting enough, sharks and marlin have been sighted here in summer months. Whew!

Stingray Reef

This large pinnacle falls short of the sea surface, its rugged top sitting in about 8 m of water, a little over one kilometre south of Ruamahuaiti Island, the southernmost island in the Alderman group. Cracks and holes are carved into the pinnacle's sloping top. As you move down the rock-face, you'll find hiwihiwi hiding in the kelp, silver drummers, marblefish, leatherjackets and red moki, and some very interesting pink sea urchins, the so-called white-spined sea urchin. The precipitous sides drop away to 30 m and are covered with colourful sponges. Scarlet wrasses and pigfish like to poke their noses into the rock-faces, while clouds of demoiselles gather in the surrounding blue water with schools of koheru and butterfly perch. Although this dive is usually much calmer than McGregor's Rock, currents can be moderate. Baby stingrays can often be found here in October and November.

Len's Reef

This is probably the prime pinnacle of the group, but it is not for the faint-hearted: it rises straight up from a 70-m sea floor about 3 km southeast of Ruamahuaiti Island. The small top – about 40 m^2 – sits in about 8 m of

water, but this pinnacle is an elongated pyramid, the base being much larger than the top. The walls are much like the other pinnacles of the area – cracked and pitted with a rainbow of invertebrate life. But the fish really make this a spectacular dive location. There are nearly always large schools of blue and pink maomao. Pelagic fish often visit the site, and divers have even seen a whale shark here.

This dive seems to be in the middle of nowhere, and it certainly is an isolated location in the middle of deep water. You truly never know what you are going to see when you get into the water here. Unfortunately, you often don't know if you can get into the water. It is difficult to find, the small apex of the pinnacle is difficult to anchor, and you really need calm conditions to dive because the currents can be strong. But strong current and isolation usually bring abundant fish life.

Homestead Reef

Location	White Island
Access	Boat
Type of dive	Reef, pinnacle, kelp
Level	Open water
Snorkel	Yes
Depth range	9–35 m
When to dive	Summer is best
Current	Slight, but can be strong on spring tides
Look for	Groups of blue moki, schools of sweep, Lord Howe coral fish

The large top of this rugged kelp-covered pinnacle to the southwest of White Island sits in about 9 m of water, and is a rocky jumble of kelp-crowned boulders. The southwest side of the pinnacle is full of ledges and, although it isn't a true vertical face, it does fall quickly to the sloping sand bottom at 35 m. Many of the rocks are smothered in encrusting sponges. Under the overhangs and recessed places created by the jumble of large rocks rest groups of large blue moki.

The first thing you will notice here is the fish life: large schools of sweep and schools of blue maomao swim among clouds of demoiselles; and schools of koheru and Spanish mackerel zoom about in mid-water. As you go deeper, you'll find lingering mobs of pink maomao, with the occasional kingfish zooming through. Around the rocks at 15–20 m deep, are Lord Howe coral fish and the usual reef fish.

Diadema Reef
Marine Reserve

Location	Underwater pinnacle off Volkner Rocks, White Island
Access	Boat
Type of dive	Pinnacle
Level	Experienced open water
Snorkel	No
Depth range	8–50 m
When to dive	Calm conditions with no wind
Current	Moderate currents, stronger on spring tides
Look for	*Diadema palmeri* sea urchins, kingfish, firebrick sea stars, sharks

This is another one of those famous east coast pinnacles that rise from the deep sea floor (in this case, 50 m). It never quite reaches the water surface but the small kelp-covered top sits in about 8 m of water. This pinnacle has one of the smallest top surfaces, so anchoring in anything but calm conditions is simply not worth the effort. But a dive at this location is definitely worth the effort.

View from Diadema Reef

Below the craggy kelp covered top there is virtually no algae; the sides of the pinnacles are steep, and the bare rugged rock faces are home to hundreds of purple sea urchins. Further down, at about 20 m, you'll find the deep crimson sea urchin, *Diadema palmeri*, for which this site is named. On the way, you'll be surrounded by thousands of blue maomao and mobs of pink maomao.

Still deeper, at about 40 m, black coral trees cling to the pinnacle's sides. This is also one of those sites where you need to keep one eye on the wall and the other out to sea. Kingfish, bronze whaler and thresher sharks have been seen here. On the way back up, look for firebrick sea stars, yellow zoanthids, nudibranchs, hydroid fans, moray eels and scorpion fish in among the rocks. You may also encounter a resident pair of Lord Howe coral fish.

Over 40 years ago, diving pioneer Bill Palmer came across a unique and new species – a brilliant red spined sea-urchin – at the Poor Knights Islands. This was the first report of *Diadema palmeri*, which is found on rocky walls in water 25–40 m deep. They have no natural predators, and are especially prolific around the Poor Knights Islands and White Island. The urchin's 'eyeball' is actually its anal sac, which is connected to its toothed mouth underneath its body.

Spanish Arch

Location	White Island
Access	Boat
Type of dive	Reef, cave, sandy bottom, kelp
Level	Open water
Snorkel	Yes
Depth range	0–16 m
When to dive	Anytime
Current	Slight
Look for	Archway, sandager wrasses, sea stars

In the middle of the western side of White Island is a small rock, called South Rock. You can swim entirely around its 350-m perimeter in a single dive. On the way, you'll find a ridge extending from the northern aspect of the island. Spanish Arch is part of this rocky formation. The top of the ridge is visible from the water surface and the archway is found at 14 m. The edge of the ceiling is encrusted with bryozoans and sponges, and half-banded perches gather here. Once upon a time, a Spanish lobster resided on the ceiling as well and unknowingly lent its name to the dive site. You can swim through the arch, and will probably spook a group of blue moki on the way in. But the demoiselles, sandager wrasses and red pigfish that live here are not so easily spooked. The other side of the arch is a kelp-covered rocky reef, the home of firebrick sea stars on the sandy sea floor. You will find the sprinters of the sea star family: the comb star.

Keep swimming with the rocky reef to your left, and you might meet other large groups of blue moki resting in the shaded areas of the reef, along with tarakihi and porae. Hammerhead sharks have also been seen here. At the southern end of the rock is a lovely shallow seaweed garden where many fish, including sandagers wrasses, black angel fish, butterfish and koheru, linger. Keep going and you come to the sheer wall of the island, and eventually a point where current flows. Here you'll find green wrasses, clouds of demoiselles; then masses of blue maomao and sweep. Soon you'll be back where you started.

Comb sea star

Lottin Point

Location	Lottin Point Bay
Access	Shore
Type of dive	Reef, sandy bottom, pinnacles
Level	Open water
Snorkel	Yes
Depth range	0–30 m
When to dive	Calm conditions; not in northerlies
Current	Can be strong around Lottin Point
Look for	Blue maomao, red moki, kingfish

You can dive right off the pohutakawa-fringed pebble beach here, although you may want to launch a small boat to get you a few hundred metres offshore, where visibility is much better. In the shallow entrance to the bay, kelp is prolific, so look out for sea urchins. Once you get to a depth of about 12–15 m (about 200 m from the shore), the kelp thins out, visibility improves, and you find yourself diving over a sandy white sea floor.

If you swim towards the point, large schools of blue maomao will buzz around you; you will see butterfly perch and red moki hovering above the rocky pinnacles; and you may be lucky to encounter inquisitive kingfish. Under the *Ecklonia* kelp that grows prolifically on the vertical rock-face, you'll find delicate lace corals, crabs, nudibranchs, and even small paua. Lottin Point itself is about 1.8 km from the beach. Here, the sea floor drops away steeply, and you'll find yourself in 50-m deep water within 100 m of the rocky shoreline.

You can drive to the beach by following a sign-posted road. There are 2 km of winding unsealed road at the end, and you pass through some farmland – leave the gates as you found them, please!

Volkner Rocks (Te Paepae Aotea) are a series of volcanic pinnacles that rise over 100 m above sea-level. Inactive today, these rocks were once part of the explosive Volcanic Plateau

of the central North Island, and are joined by a 200-m deep submarine saddle to White Island, just 5 km away.

Carl Völkner was a tenacious missionary who, in 1865, ignored warnings and decided to challenge the Maori of Opotiki, who had cast aside their Christian beliefs in favour of Hau Hauism (a combination of Christianity and traditional Maori beliefs). Völkner was hung from a tree and eventually decapitated. Legend tells that a Hau Hau prophet then preached to his followers from a pulpit with Völkner's head at his side, and that at one point he plucked out Völkner's eyeballs and swallowed them.

Not so long ago the pinnacles were fired upon as target practice by the New Zealand military. Today, the rocks and seas that surround them are peaceful and protected as a marine reserve.

Bay of Plenty and the east coast of the North Island

Cook
Strait

Siren's Reef

Wellington south coast

Cook Strait's unpredictable reputation is second to none. At its narrowest, the waterway that separates the two main islands of New Zealand is just 23 km wide, yet the journey across can seem interminable when the seas and southerly gales are roaring past Marlborough to the east and Wellington to the west. The North and South islands were once joined, but rising sea-levels flooded the low-lying strip of land, forming what we now know as Cook Strait. Also flooded were the valleys of the northeastern edge of the South Island – the Marlborough Sounds. Nature has sculpted the top of the South Island into myriad islands, rocks, bays and passages.

Abel Tasman first discovered the western aspect of the strait in 1642, but believed the eastern aspect to be landlocked. At the time, Tasman noted a possibility of an eastern opening due to water movement, but he didn't probe further. Over 100 years later, Captain James Cook, in whose honour the strait is named, commenced where Tasman left off and successfully navigated the waterway from the Tasman Sea to Pacific Ocean in 1769. Of course, Maori had been navigating these waters, which they call Raukawa Moana (Sea of bitter leaves) for many years.

104

Blue Cod

Blue cod (*Parapercis colias*, pakirikiri/ rawaru) are not actually part of the cod family, despite their name. They live only around New Zealand and, although they are found on the rocky sea floor around the North Island, they are really a southern fish, being particularly abundant in the Marlborough Sounds. Blue cod are commonly caught and eaten in the South Island, but they are under serious threat from over-fishing. Juvenile blue cod are brown: they change to mottled grey-green and eventually blue in full adult form. Blue cod, all of which start off as females, can live for up to 20 years, growing to 60–70 cm in length and weighing 3–4 km.

Kapiti Island, to the north of the strait, was once the place of marine mammal slaughter – southern right whales were killed and processed on the island until 1847. Now, the island is a nature reserve and all of the land-dwelling animals and birds are fully protected. In addition, about half of the coastline and a little over 2000 ha of the water surrounding the island are included in a marine reserve. The reserve extends eastward back to an estuary on the mainland, providing a unique corridor between the two that many marine animals exploit. Kapiti Island is an important breeding ground for a number of New Zealand native birds, and visitors to the island marvel at

Wellington south coast

the diversity of species found there. Underwater, the meeting of the cold southern and warmer northern currents has resulted in an equally unique mix of species. The best dive sites are located on the northern and western shores, but snorkelling along any accessible coastline will be rewarding.

Cook Strait has always been a busy waterway. Maori traversed it in flotillas of waka and, for centuries, whales have passed through on their annual north–south migrations. The whales attracted many Europeans to the area in the early nineteenth century, and shipping traffic hasn't

Marlborough Sounds

diminished since. But the tumultuous seas have claimed over 100 ships in a little over 150 years. Passenger ferries, cruise ships, wooden sailing ships and steamers have all succumbed to the strait's might. The convoluted waterways of Marlborough Sounds are remarkably calm, and have provided much needed refuge for mariners, ancient and modern, from the strait.

The large and far-reaching Cook Strait is home to many and varied dive sites, including many shipwrecks. But you don't have to venture far from Wellington city to enjoy some of the strait's best diving. Proximity to a city usually means murky inshore waters and limited underwater life, but the constant battering by turbulent seas keeps the southern shoreline of the North Island interesting, and there are great dive locations just minutes from Wellington city and its busy port. However, just as the seas of Cook Strait are legendary, so too is Wellington's wind. When the southerlies are blowing, you'll find it hard to get into the water near the city. But when they stop blowing, you'll find the submerged rocks of Wellington's southern coastline covered in prolific life, thriving in the rich seas that only a steady, replenishing current can provide. It is difficult to imagine a capital city anywhere in the world that is so perfectly poised for underwater exploration.

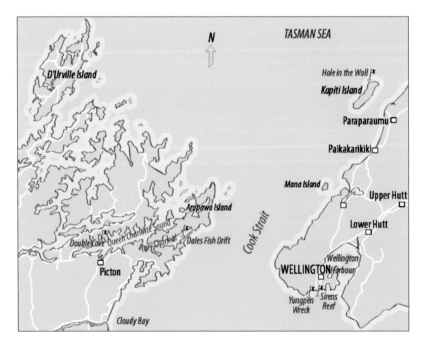

Cook Strait

Diving Cook Strait

Underwater conditions vary greatly throughout the waters of Cook Strait. Expect temperatures of around 10–12°C (50–54°F) during winter and 16°C (61°F) during the summer months. Around Kapiti Island, the water temperature is usually 1–2 degrees warmer: 18°C (64°F) in summer and 12°C (54°F) in winter. Underwater visibility varies in the region: expect typically about 3–6 m along Wellington's southern coast; 5 m in winter and 15–20 m in summer around Kapiti Island; and 8 m in winter and 6 m in summer around Picton. Generally, the further from the coast into open water you venture, the clearer the water.

Marlborough Sounds

Hole in the Wall

Marine Reserve

Location	Arapawaiti Point, western Kapiti Island Marine Reserve
Access	Boat
Type of dive	Reef, pebbly bottom, wall, cave, kelp
Level	Open water
Snorkel	Yes
Depth range	0–20 m
When to dive	Only mild swell; afternoon
Current	Slight to moderate, can be very turbulent in east entrance
Look for	Jewel anemones, butterfly perch, butterfish, crayfish, blue cod

Above Kapiti Island Marine Reserve, the northern peninsula of Kapiti Island is craggy and steep. Approaching from the eastern side, an incomplete archway is visible above water, and about 2–3 m beneath the water is the narrow cave entrance. When you enter the water, you won't see much more than a dense kelp meadow. Gliding over *Ecklonia* kelp-covered boulders in the bay towards the cave entrance, crayfish wave their antennae inquisitively outwards. As you approach the kelp, butterfish will zip here and there; curious blue cod will ogle you; and the occasional red moki scoots past.

The underwater cave entrance, flanked by large boulders to the left, is on a vertical wall. Swimming into the tunnel is like entering a washing machine

as the turbulent water flows from the wider tunnel through the narrow exit. The dense invertebrate life lining the cave walls and huge boulders are a vivid reminder that current flows through this passage often and fast. Once you pass the boulders, the water settles down and the boulders are replaced by a 9-m deep pebble sea floor leading you through a spacious 20-m tunnel to the western side of the peninsula. Jewel anemones have colonised every available surface, creating a fluorescent carpet of yellow, orange and brilliant pink.

Emerging on the western side of the peninsula, rock pinnacles, each with a crown of *Ecklonia* kelp, lead towards the sea floor. Crayfish shelter in between the boulder landscape that is covered with more jewel anemones and luminescent yellow zoanthids. Hundreds of butterfly perch feed in mid-water or hover over the rocky pinnacles. Swimming to the right, around the headland, will lead back to the start of this colourful and energetic dive.

Siren's Reef
Proposed Marine Reserve

Location	Owhiro Bay, south coast, Wellington
Access	Shore
Type of dive	Reef, pebble and boulder bottom
Level	Open water
Snorkel	Yes
Depth range	0–10 m
Current	Slight
When to dive	Northerly conditions; slight southern swell at most; outgoing high tide
Look for	Triplefins, algae, anemones

As soon as you enter the water at Owhiro Bay, you'll notice the rich aquatic landscape. Full of different algae and invertebrate life, the waters will inevitably become home to many fish with passing time and protection.

The dive begins by wading between two rocky outcrops, directly from the beach at high tide. Before you have gone very far, you'll notice the large warratah anemones clinging to the eastern channel walls.

The dive site is essentially a huge lagoon with submerged rocky outcrops, running perpendicular to the shoreline, like long undulating fingers leading to the deeper waters of Cook Strait. These sculpted and undercut rocky shapes, which lie just 1–2 m below the sea surface, are separated by 7–10-m deep valleys with pebble and boulder floors.

Every part of this rocky landscape is covered with life: the sea-smoothed boulders blush with candy pink coralline algae, pink and white anemones and clusters of brightly coloured jewel anemones. This colourful boulder landscape is home to many juvenile fish, such as butterfish, wrasse and moki, while the calm lagoon is the perfect place to observe the lives of triplefins and sea stars.

Cook Strait

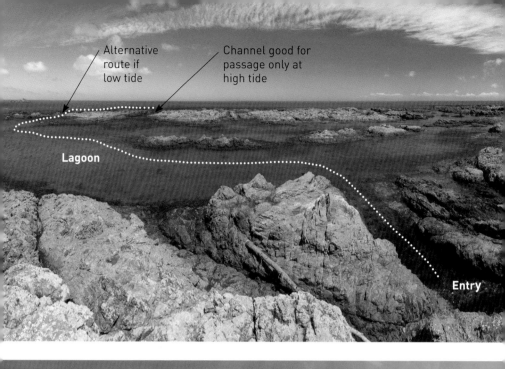

Alternative route if low tide

Channel good for passage only at high tide

Lagoon

Entry

The *Yung Pen* Shipwreck
Proposed Marine Reserve

Location	Owhiro Bay, south coast, Wellington
Access	Shore
Type of dive	Reef, wreck, sandy bottom
Level	Open water
Snorkel	Yes
Depth range	0–10 m
When to dive	Northerly conditions; slight southern swell at most; outgoing tide
Current	Moderate to strong
Look for	Blue moki, blue cushion stars, algae

The *Yung Pen*, a Japanese steel fishing trawler, came to its end one dark December night in 1982. The ship came adrift in the early hours of the morning and was too close to the rocky coast to be salvaged once its peril was discovered. This strangely attractive area has also claimed three other victims: the *Wellington*, a 153-ft wooden sailing ship that sank here in 1874 during a horrific storm; the *Cyrus*, a 119-ft three-masted barque that sank during the same stormy night; and the *Progress*, a 129-ft iron steamer that endured a similar fate in 1931 after losing its propeller. The *Yung Pen* is the most intact of the vessels: the other three wrecks' broken and scattered remains are difficult to locate. It is also the most interesting to dive.

An old concrete boat ramp leads you down to the start of this dive, a narrow channel leading to a large lagoon. The lagoon's pebbly floor is full of life: blue cod, juvenile blue moki and cushion sea stars graze among the beds of bright green lettuce and red algae.

About 50 m from the coast and along the lagoon's southern aspect are two long, visible rocky islands. Between these two, the *Yung Pen* lies upside down in the 9-m deep channel. A few recognisable parts of the *Progress*, including its boiler, can be found on the outside and to the east of the channel. Hundreds

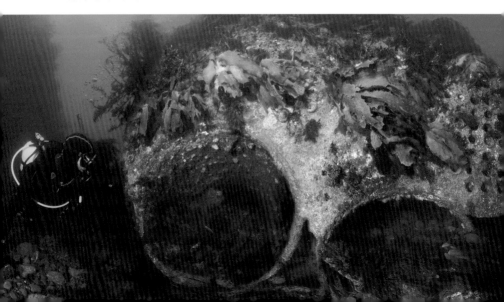

Boilers from
the *Progress*

Yung Pen

Lagoon

Lagoon
Channel

Old boat
ramp

of shiny, spiky stainless steel jigs are scattered across the pebbles and gravel that make up the sea floor. Thousands of these squid-catching jigs were once stored onboard the *Yung Pen*, a squid-fishing vessel, which has now been taken over by paua, crayfish and algae. Rose-coloured coralline algae cover almost every surface, and the sides of the wreck are covered with rimu seaweed, *Caulerpa brownii*. The uppermost surface of the wreck, just a couple of metres below the high-tide line, has been colonised by *Ecklonia* kelp.

In a little over 25 years, the man-made structure has become the skeleton for a rich and varied reef, which is now home to large marblefish and small schools of blue moki. Throughout the next 25 years, fish life will increase further once the no-take marine reserve comes into effect.

Double Cove
Restricted fishing area

Location	Double Cove, Queen Charlotte Sound
Access	Boat
Type of dive	Wreck, sandy bottom, kelp forest, drift
Level	Open water
Snorkel	Yes
Depth range	8–14 m
When to dive	Anytime, but not after heavy rain
Current	None
Look for	Blue cod, tube worms, yellow-eyed mullet, sea horses, camouflage crabs, nudibranchs

Double Cove Fishing Restricted Area was established in 1986 and, although the area is not a full marine reserve, the fact that fishing has been banned for over 20 years is apparent when you enter the water. The shallow bay has a couple of great attractions – a well-seasoned wreck to explore and the cod hole, which, as its name suggests, is the gathering place of local cod.

This shallow dive gives you a taste of what a typical New Zealand coastal environment might be like if fishing were restricted. This mostly empty seascape is home to a huge number of blue cod. Not only are they plentiful, but these are the biggest, fattest and friendliest blue cod you are likely to encounter around New Zealand's coastline. They share these calm waters with schools of yellow-eyed mullet that also appear to be larger than their usual size. Sea urchins graze on the sparse kelp that grows on a sea floor that appears barren at first glance. However, closer inspection reveals mountains of tube-worm colonies and sea squirts clinging to rocky surfaces.

Koi shipwreck

About 50 m offshore from a sandy beach between Torea Point and Double Cove lies the *Koi* shipwreck, a 26-m vessel that was originally built in Scotland, but shipped to New Zealand where she was reassembled in 1906. The Koi, which served as a passenger ferry around Motueka then a coal hulk in later years, was

Koi shipwreck   Cod Hole   Cod Hole

swamped in 1910, but successfully refloated. However, after sinking on her mooring at Picton in 1940, she was towed to and sunk at her final resting place. With no major trauma, the ship fell almost straight down and lies almost upright on the 12-m sea floor. Time has eaten away the wooden deck, but the hull, engines and engine room are intact.

Divers follow the mooring line to the stern: visibility is not the best, about 3–4 m, but the hulk of the characteristic hull shape is unmistakable arising from the mostly shell sea floor. Not that you can distinguish any of the original steel hull, because the ship has been completely taken over by a dense garden of algae. Squeezed in between are all kinds of invertebrates, sea urchins, eleven-armed sea stars and nudibranchs. In perfect camouflage, decorator crabs scramble unseen over the ship's hull, while sea horses cling to algae. Blue cod and spotties are always close by.

Cod Hole

Koi shipwreck

Mikhail Lermontov

One of the more recent maritime victims of the strait was the *Mikhail Lermontov*, a luxury Russian passenger liner that sank in 1986. Over 150 m long and weighing 20,000 tons, the vessel was fatally crippled when rocks ripped apart its hull as the captain tried to manoeuvre through a narrow passage near Cape Jackson. Remarkably, all but one of the 738 people aboard survived. The nearly intact and penetrable ship lies on her side in 30–40 m of water. Unfortunately, this is not one of New Zealand's most accessible or easiest dives, as sea conditions are often less than perfect, and it is a deep dive that is subject to current.

Cook Strait

Pete Mesley

Dale's Fish Drift

Location	Tory Channel, Marlborough Sounds
Access	Boat
Type of dive	Reef, sandy bottom, kelp
Level	Open water
Snorkel	Yes
Depth range	0–20 m
When to dive	Slack water; full sun
Current	Moderate
Look for	*Macrocystis pyrifera* (giant kelp) trees, butterfish, blue moki, spotties

Drift dives are always an adventure, as you move effortlessly through the water with the current. Many drift dives are fast and furious, but, when a slowish current takes you on a meander through a giant kelp forest that is teeming with schools of fish, it can be extraordinary. Dale's Fish Drift takes you on a journey through Tory Channel, the main waterway to Picton. It is a fairly shallow (5–10 m) drift through a *Macrocystis* kelp forest where thousands of active spotties buzz around you, and large butterfish and blue moki weave their way through the buoyant trees. Brushing aside the rubbery limbs reveals the holdfasts that do exactly that – secure the tall kelp trees to the rocks. An inspection of the holdfasts and rocks reveals a collection of invertebrates, triplefins, bright jewel anemones, sea tulips and encrusting sponges. This colourful palette is interlaced with the green grapeweed, *Caulerpa geminata*. Venture a little deeper, and the kelp gives way to a gently sloping sand bottom, where you may encounter large schools of fish, including hundreds of butterfly fish.

Cook Strait

This dive is surprisingly calm given it is located in a major harbour thoroughfare. The dense kelp fronds form a ceiling on the water surface above, creating a tunnel effect beneath. When the full sun penetrates the gaps between the leaves, the dazzling light show beneath creates a magical underwater location. When a huge passenger or car ferry passes through – at a very safe distance, of course - the underwater roar jolts your senses. But a few minutes later, when the calm returns, the ship's wake makes the light rays dance.

Lower South Island
and Stewart Island

Northeastern side of Half Moon Bay, Stewart Island

The South Island's long eastern coastline offers plenty of easy water access and, with few towns creating run-off, the water is clear and inviting – not just to us, but to ocean wildlife as well. It's a natural haven for many

marine species: New Zealand sealions breed unchallenged on Otago's southern beaches and royal albatross can be seen gliding to their breeding ground on Taiaroa Head. This heavily guarded site at the entrance to Otago Harbour is the world's only mainland breeding colony of these giant ocean gliders. Spending most of their lives at sea, royal albatrosses, with their 3.3 m wingspan, travel close to 200,000 km a year, between their southern ocean feeding grounds and their breeding grounds.

Captain Cook and the *Endeavour* crew hunted albatrosses as they crossed the southern seas, before circumnavigating and mapping the New Zealand coastline. They made few mistakes, but two major ones in relation to the South Island: Stewart Island was attached to the South Island, and Banks Peninsula (named after the ship's botanist, Joseph Banks) was separated from it. Nor did they land – that was left to the crew of a European whaling vessel, who are believed to be the first Europeans to land at Akaroa on Banks Peninsula around 1815. By the 1840s, the peninsula was a busy whaling area with several stations. Now the whales and other sea mammals are strictly protected around New Zealand's coast, and even more so around Banks Peninsula, where New Zealand's first marine mammal sanctuary has been established. This was done primarily to protect the endangered population of Hector's dolphins in the area, but all marine cetaceans have benefited.

Further north, the small town of Kaikoura is the marine capital of New Zealand. It is a marine wildlife watcher's dream come true. Sperm whales, humpback whales in season, Hector's dolphins, Dusky dolphins and New Zealand fur seals play and feed just a short boat ride from the shore. Kaikoura's secret is the Hikurangi Trench. Invisible to the human eye, this deep underwater canyon – with a 2000-m deep

Kaikoura

Te Waikoropupu Springs (Pupu Springs)

Pupu Springs, at the top of the South Island, have a flow of 14,000 l of very cold water (11.7°C) every second. Scientists have assessed underwater horizontal visibility in the main spring to be 63 m, which is close to the theoretical maximum for optically pure water. This pure water upsurges through fine white sand and supports a dense array of aquatic plants. The springs used to be the ultimate in freshwater dives, but they are now closed to divers to prevent the spread of invasive introduced weeds that have already taken over some New Zealand rivers. We hope they will open again one day. In the meantime, there is an underwater viewing platform, and the springs remain worthy of a visit.

sea floor – is the territory of ferocious-looking angler fish, creepy-looking hagfish, huge and weird-looking crustaceans and, of course, the elusive giant squid. The deep canyon is teeming with life – from microscopic plankton to giant mammals. The profusion of life attracts more life in a self-perpetuating cycle. Daily, divers take the rare opportunity to snorkel with dolphins and swim with seals, with almost guaranteed certainty that both will be encountered.

Green Island, Dunedin

Dunedin's long harbour is great place to start diving in the South Island. The coastal sea floor is relatively shallow and flat – the drop-off occurs about 30 km offshore, where the sea floor descends steeply. This marks the ancient edge of the Otago coast that disappeared about the same time the valley leading to the site of Dunedin city was flooded. There is also an incredible man-made structure at the entrance to Otago Harbour – The Mole – that definitely should be explored.

At the very bottom of New Zealand is Stewart Island, where kiwi outnumber people 50 to 1, and walking tracks outnumber roads 10 to 1. Known as Rakiura, or land of the glowing skies in Maori, the island is as close to natural as anywhere might be, and 85 per cent of its landmass is now a protected national park. Giant kelp forests prosper in the deep, clear oceanic waters. In fact, Stewart Island has more types of seaweed than anywhere else in New Zealand – close to 400 different red, brown and green algae. Look closely and you will also find ancient brachipods, a rarity shared with Fiordland. Another Fiordland local, the crested penguin nests on nearby Codfish Island with New Zealand's two other penguins: little blue and yellow-eyed.

The South Island is a land of plenty – plenty of space, plenty of ocean and plenty of wildlife. The South Island also encompasses Fiordland, another unique New Zealand diving location, which is the subject of the next chapter. Enjoy the isolation and the unique encounters with marine life throughout the South Island.

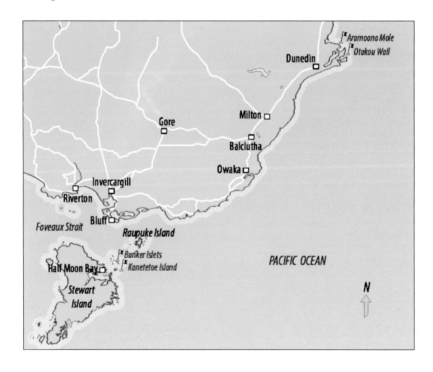

Lower South Island and Stewart Island

Diving down south

Underwater visibility around the South Island will vary depending on how close you are to large rivers. Expect 8–16 m at Stewart Island during summer and 10–12 m in winter, with clearer water as you head further offshore. The water temperature around Stewart Island ranges from 10-12°C (50–54°F) between May and September, and 12–15°C (54–59°F) between January and April. Otago Harbour visibility ranges from 2–10 m, with a winter water temperature of 8–10°C (46–50°F) and a summer temperature of 12–15°C (54–59°F).

Kaikoura

Otakou Wall

Location	Shipping channel, off Harington Point, Otago Harbour
Access	Boat
Type of dive	Sloping seabed
Level	Open water
Snorkel	No
Depth range	10–22 m
When to dive	Diving must be authorised by the Otago Port Authority; contact the local dive shop, Dive Otago, for more details
Current	Strong current; can be done as a drift dive or at slack water
Look for	Sponges, invertebrates

Otago Harbour is a busy place. In 2004, 537 vessels visited the harbour's two ports – Port Chalmers and Port Otago at Dunedin – where 2.8 million tons of cargo was handled. New Zealand's very first export of frozen meat left Port Chalmers in 1882. It arrived in London 98 days later, marking the beginning of New Zealand's very successful agricultural export trade. Dunedin is 12 km away from the sea, and the wide Otago Harbour is actually a submerged valley that is prone to silting up. The harbour is dredged from time to time to allow big ships through, so it is difficult to imagine choosing to dive in the centre of all this traffic. Although the

dredging may damage the sponge garden, it will grow back. And yet, this is really a very unique dive.

The visibility is not great – expect 1.5 m at the worst and 5 m when it's good – and you will not be disappointed. Once you find the bottom in the blue-green gloom, you'll find an exquisite rainbow sponge garden. Orange and pink encrusting sponges cling to any structure they can, while finger sponges gently sway in the moving waters. Other colourful invertebrates growing between including ascidians, bryozoans and anemones. Lots of creatures make their home here, including the rather large black shield slug, *Scutus*. The combination of poor visibility and dense invertebrate colonies makes it easy to forget you're diving in a busy harbour. But when a sea lion swims so close that you can see it, as they often do at this dive site, you're jolted back into reality.

Yellow-eyed penguin/ hoiho (*Megadyptes antipodes*), the third largest penguin in the world, lives on the South Island, as well as Stewart, Campbell and Auckland islands. One of the world's rarest penguins, they can be seen tottering towards the water each dawn and back to their nests each dusk from Banks Peninsula to the Catlin's coastline in South Otago, but especially around Dunedin and Oamaru. Unlike other penguins, which rejoice in large noisy colonies, hoiho prefer solitude, and often nest very far from each other in the grass and flax of the foreshore. In their quest for privacy, they may slowly waddle up to one kilometre from the water's edge. If you are lucky to see one of them underwater, they'll whiz past you at speeds of up to 25 kph, dive deeper than you to 120 m and swim up to 40 km offshore.

Aramoana Mole

Location	Aramoana, North side of Otago Harbour entrance
Access	Shore
Type of dive	Manmade wall, shipwrecks
Level	Open water
Snorkel	No
Depth range	7– 22 m
When to dive	Not in north or northeasterly conditions
Current	Slight
Look for	Shipwrecks, invertebrates

The Aramoana Mole is undoubtedly New Zealand's first man-made artificial reef and underwater structure. In 1884, just as shipping was becoming a regular feature of Otago Harbour, the decision was made to build two sea walls to redirect water entering the entrance of the harbour and prevent the build-up of silt. The first stage of building included ramming huge black-pine poles into the sea floor, a task partly achieved with prison labour. Joists were built across the top and a railway used to ferry locally quarried rocks to the growing pier, where they were dumped into a framework to form a wall. Within a year, the Mole was 304 m long and 12 m wide, and it kept growing. But, although the shore end was above the high tideline, the outer edge was some 4.5 m below high tide. Over the years, the Mole has suffered fire, theft of its visible wood and, of course, the force of the sea. Attempts have been made to rebuild it many times, but none has been totally successful.

Mokoia shipwreck

Lower South Island and Stewart Island

Mokoia shipwreck

Since 1926, several ships have been scuttled along the harbour side of the Mole, at first just to get rid of them, and later to help protect the underwater structure. Today, there is literally a chain of wrecks lying almost parallel with the Mole itself. You need to plan several dives in the area to fully explore all of the wrecks and the wall itself. Decades, and in some cases nearly a century, underwater have left them virtually covered with dense invertebrate life. Bladder kelp (*Macrocystis pyrifera*) is common and may extend all the way to the sea surface. Many different types of algae can be found, including the encrusting coralline algae, but other leafy red algae are common as well. Filter-feeding sea tulips sway gently on their long stalks, while fat sea stars slowly crawl over the ships' surfaces.

132

Some of the ships have cavernous spaces that you can swim through. Many fish take advantage of these spaces – it is not uncommon to find groups of fish, such as blue moki, hiding in the hull of an old ship.

Paloona shipwreck

Kanetetoe Island

Location	Fancy Islands, northeast Titi Islands, off Stewart Island
Access	Boat
Type of dive	Boulders, pinnacles
Level	Open water
Snorkel	No
Depth range	0–20 m
When to dive	On small tides or slack water
Current	Strong
Look for	Large schools of fish, shells, sea tulips

This island is part of the Fancy Island group of the northeast Titi, or Muttonbird, Islands that lie approximately 10 km from Half Moon Bay on

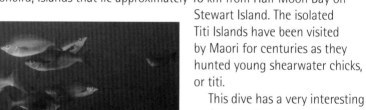

Stewart Island. The isolated Titi Islands have been visited by Maori for centuries as they hunted young shearwater chicks, or titi.

This dive has a very interesting underwater landscape. You'll find big boulders scattered across the bottom and, in between, pinnacles thrusting upwards from the sea floor. Everything is covered with life: the kelp is luxuriant and varied, and the fish are large and plentiful. Big groups of trumpeters, blue moki, girdled and banded wrasses, and hundreds of large telescope share their home with sea tulips and masses of sea urchins. Closer inspection of the bryozoan and sponge gardens will reveal nudibranchs, tiny triplefins and tiger shells.

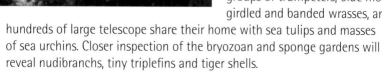

Lower South Island and Stewart Island

Kanetetoe Island

Hector's Dolphin

Hector's Dolphin (*Cephalorhynchus hectori*), the smallest dolphin in the world, lives only in the coastal waters of New Zealand's South Island. Hector's dolphins, named after Sir James Hector, a renowned scientist who first described them, are often seen in shallow coastal waters (less than 20 m deep) and rarely swim deeper than 100 m. As a result, there are west and east coast South Island populations that never meet, separated as they are by stretches of deep water they never traverse. Even more isolated is the Hector's cousin, Maui's dolphin that lives on the North Island's west coast. Maui's dolphin was identified as a genetically different species in 2002 and is the rarest dolphin in the world – they are critically endangered, with an estimated total population of just 100 living animals remaining.

Lower South Island and Stewart Island

Bunker Islets

Location	Northeast Titi Islands, off Stewart Island
Access	Boat
Type of dive	Seal
Level	Open water
Snorkel	Yes
Depth range	0–5 m
When to dive	Anytime
Current	None
Look for	Seals

Most of the residents of Stewart Island are descended directly from either the original Maori inhabitants of the island, or from nineteenth-century European whalers and sealers who worked in the area. New Zealand fur seals, one of only two types of land mammals indigenous to New Zealand, were hunted to near extinction, but today breeding colonies flourish all around southern New Zealand. The Bunker Islets is the location of one of the area's seal-breeding colonies.

The rocky shore that rims the bay is scattered with dark mounds: the sleeping adult seals that are, at best, indifferent as divers enter the water near their offspring. Small, sleek bodies of the seal pups lumber onto rocks and launch themselves, with a small splash, back into the sea. Underwater, it doesn't seem to matter whether you are on scuba or just snorkelling, their mesmerising display occurs before your eyes. Speeding, diving, bending, rolling and twisting: these energetic mammals never seem to run out of energy or enthusiasm for their play. They are playful and tactile with each other, and with their new friends – divers. They seem as interested in us as we are in them. This is one of the best wildlife encounters you will ever have.

Fiordland

Mitre Peak, Milford Sound

Fiordland is New Zealand's number one tourist destination, with half a million people visiting Milford Sound every year. But how many venture underwater? There are lots of excuses for *not* getting wet: it's cold; it's difficult to transport all your dive gear; there's a high mountain pass to traverse on the way out; and the layer of freshwater looks murky and not particularly inviting. But there are many more reasons to venture beneath these still waterways.

To Maori, who came to the area to hunt and gather precious pounamu (greenstone), the fiords have always held special significance. But could these people ever have imagined what lay beneath the water? The unexplored underwater environment is bathed in perpetual twilight: it's a place where black coral, as well as dolphins, seals and penguins, thrive.

Ancient glaciers have sculpted the southwest corner of the South Island. The 14 fingers of the Tasman Sea that dissect the coast and forest were first described by Captain Cook in 1770. The *Endeavour* crew made a surprisingly accurate first map of the area, but didn't venture very far into the fiords themselves. Three years later, on the *Resolution*, Captain Cook and a new crew navigated the waterways and named (incorrectly) most of the fiords as sounds. These early European visitors encountered a large resident fur seal population. Twenty years later, the waterways were busy with sealers; 30 years later the seals were nearly extinct. Today, seals bask safely on the rocky edge of the water that they share with penguins, dolphins and plenty of fish.

Fiordland's precipitous mountains continue their downward plunge as

Fiords or Sounds?

Fiords and sounds are defined by their underwater architecture. Sounds are flooded valleys that descend gradually to the sea floor. Fiords are carved by glaciers and have a distinctive U shape, with a wall of rock separating the deep water from that of the adjoining open sea. As a result, depending on the sea-level, the saltwater is trapped in the fiord, and is very clear and often relatively still. The European explorers who named Fiordland's waterways could not have anticipated what the underwater structure looked like.

they pass through the waterline, extending to the deep water hundreds of metres below. Clinging to these near vertical walls are anemones, corals, sponges and majestic black coral trees – all at much shallower and more achievable diving depths than other places around New Zealand. The fiords are believed to contain the world's biggest population of black coral trees, literally millions of individual colonies. Fiordland is also home to ancient brachiopods, or lamp shells. Evolution has overlooked these primitive clam-like animals that have remained unchanged for 300 million years. The calm waterways are protected on almost all sides by mountains, and at the ocean entrance by a deep underwater ridge.

Acheron Passage, Dusky Sound

Milford Sound's Mitre Peak is undoubtedly one the most recognised mountains in New Zealand. And Milford Sound is a busy place, with many fishing and tourist boats using the small waterfront area. Milford Sound is also home to a unique underwater observatory, where you descend into a reverse fish tank – you're captive; the fish are not. Although Milford Sound is the most visited of the fiords, Doubtful Sound is the second largest and one of the longest. The head of Doubtful Sound is some 40 km away from the Tasman Sea. As the *Endeavour* sailed past the entrance to Doubtful Sound, Cook was doubtful there would be enough wind to sail out again. He never made the journey up the sound on any of his New Zealand voyages. Doubtful and Milford sounds are home to Fiordland's first marine reserves: established in 1993, there are now 10 altogether.

Shelter Islands, Doubtful Sound

Breaksea Sound

An essential ingredient of Fiordland's underwater environment is the legendary rainfall. After flowing through and over the fertile ground, the tannin-rich, honey-coloured, freshwater floats above the deep saltwater in an undisturbed layer, filtering much of the sunlight and creating an ethereal green glow underwater. The ever-present freshwater layer varies from a few centimetres to several metres deep, creating an ever-changing tidal zone for the shallow species that live here, as well as affecting the degree of sunlight filtered through to the seawater and animals below. Algae and creatures have evolved in the perpetual twilight to live at shallower depths than they might otherwise live. In fact, most of Fiordland's marine life exists in the top 40 m of water, in a thin band around the tortuous coastline. Wherever you dive in Fiordland you will feel isolated, and you'll most likely be the only divers around.

144

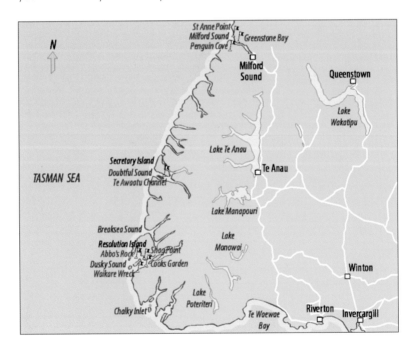

Fiordland

Diving in Fiordland

Day trips are available in Milford Sound and overnight trips in Doubtful Sound; but to really explore the fiords, you should join a live-aboard charter. Coastal access is non-existent. The more isolated fiords offer wonderful diving, but are difficult to get to. We have chosen dive sites that are for the most part easily accessible and offer a range of diving. There is almost always a layer of tannin-stained freshwater that sits on top of the saltwater. This may be minimal – less than 30 cm – or up to 15 m deep. Typically, it is just a few metres, but is enough to reduce the amount of light passing through, and turn the underwater landscape an emerald green. The freshwater layer is murky, and where it meets the saltwater especially so. Beneath this, underwater visibility improves but does vary: expect 15–20 m, but sometimes it will be over 30 m. Water temperatures are around 8–11°C (46–52°F) in winter and 15–20°C (59–68°F) in summer.

Milford Sound

Te Awaatu Channel (The Gut)
Marine Reserve

Location	Doubtful Sound
Access	Boat
Type of dive	Wall and sand bottom
Level	Experienced open water
Snorkel	No
Depth range	0–40 m
When to dive	Slack water
Current	Moderate to strong
Look for	Sea pens, zoanthids, red hydrocoral

This 200-m wide channel that lies between Bauza Island and the steep Secretary Island in Doubtful Sound was one of the first marine reserves to be established within Fiordland in 1993. Unlike some locations in Fiordland,

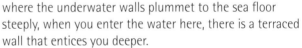

where the underwater walls plummet to the sea floor steeply, when you enter the water here, there is a terraced wall that entices you deeper.

These 20-m deep terraces are home to depth-determined bands of life: bright green algae lead to coralline algae, to sponge gardens and zoanthid beds, to small red hydrocorals and spreading black coral trees. Invertebrate life and mussels are plentiful, as are the voracious sea stars wandering among the mussel shell remnants of their feeding. Crayfish, blue cod and sea perch will be found on the rocky surfaces.

Following the terraces down to 30 m or so will lead to a barren sea floor of sand. Barren, that is, but for the extraordinarily ornate sea pens, filter-feeders that gorge in response to passing current. Continuing on, a dim shape appears on the edge of visibility – a rocky reef that glows yellow with a dense covering of yellow zoanthids. As you get closer, you notice the stark contrast of brittle red hydrocorals and small black coral trees sprinkled among this carpet of flower-like animals.

The Gut

The Gut

Greenstone Bay

Location	Milford Sound
Access	Boat
Type of dive	Wall
Level	Open water
Snorkel	No
Depth range	0–40+ m
When to dive	Not in north-northeasterly conditions
Current	Slight
Look for	Red hydrocorals, large black coral trees, orange lace bryozoans

This dive, located on the southern side of Milford Sound in a previously lucrative pounamu-gathering place, is essentially a wall dive – a vertical, seemingly never-ending wall that plummets to unseen depths. Above water the overhanging trees cling to the uneven land, while just below the tide, red algae clings to the undulating rocks that lead divers first through mussel beds.

Swimming with the land to your left, you'll pass delicate colonies of orange bryozoans, commonly called lace corals, at about 4–5 m deep, and notice schools of banded wrasse gathering around you. Then at about 16 m, you'll find red hydrocorals and tube anemones in pockets of sand in one of the rocky ledges. You can dive as deep as you want on the wall, but you won't have to go far to find really large black coral trees, yellow finger sponges and yellow gorgonian fans. Snake sea stars are

commonly seen entwined around the black coral trees, and 11-armed sea stars will inevitably be found grazing on the mussel beds. Sea perch and crayfish stay close to the wall, whereas marblefish and banded wrasse swim above the underwater terrain.

This is one of the fishiest dives in Milford Sound, and the black coral trees are some of the biggest you will ever see. Black coral trees have their own micro-ecosystem around them – animals that gather to take advantage of the natural filtration of the rich seas. Even the perishing black coral trees provide a skeleton around which other animals can base their lives.

Brachiopods

Once abundant throughout the world's oceans, brachiopods are now extremely rare and found only in cold, deep water close to the polar regions of the world; and, of course, Fiordland. Living animals of today very rarely resemble the ancient fossils that are said to be their ancestors. What is most remarkable about brachiopods is that, since they first appeared 500 million years ago, their simple clam-like structure has remained almost completely unchanged – they have evaded evolution and are essentially living fossils.

Fiordland

Penguin Cove
Marine Reserve

Location	Piopiotahi Marine Reserve, Dale Point, Milford Sound
Access	Boat
Type of dive	Wall, sandy bottom with scattered boulders
Level	Open water
Snorkel	No
Depth range	0–30 m
When to dive	Anytime except strong northerlies
Current	Slight
Look for	Huge boulders, black coral trees, snake sea stars, stargazer, tube anemones

This 690-ha marine reserve was established in 1993, and was one of the first reserves in Fiordland's waterways. The start of this dive is much like many others in Fiordland – there is a near-vertical wall with black coral trees extending into the sea at characteristic right angles. Butterfly perch congregate around the trees, which are festooned with sea stars. But as you descend further, and swim around the bay with the land to your left, the wall flattens out and leads you to a quite barren sandy sea floor. All across this landscape lie fallen trees – the after-effects of landslides above – with a few boulders scattered in between. Most have a solitary black coral tree growing, uncharacteristically, upright. The large bay is dotted with these solitary specimens.

Swimming on, you'll encounter a truck-sized rock crowned with *Ecklonia* kelp sitting in the middle of the bay. Further along is another anemone-covered rock, balanced a perfect height above the sea floor to provide shelter for crayfish and butterfly perch in the otherwise barren bay. As the sea floor slopes away to the depths, stargazers, tube anemones and clusters of horse mussels are scattered across the empty landscape. Ascending back towards the shallows at the end of the dive, the invertebrate life returns – walls of daisy anemones and blue sponges cling to the rocks, as do rimu weed and other algae.

St Anne Point

St Anne Point

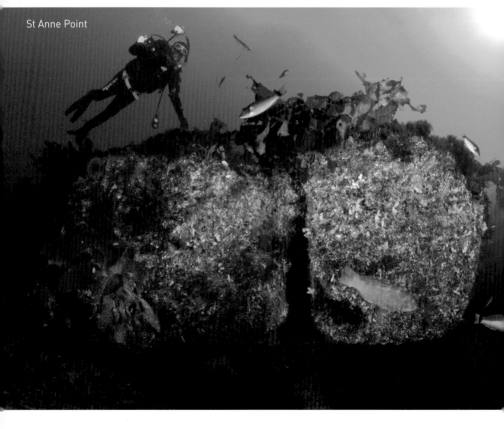
St Anne Point

St Anne Point

Location	Entrance to Milford Sound
Access	Boat
Type of dive	Wall and boulder bottom
Level	Open water
Snorkel	Yes
Depth range	0–40 m
When to dive	Anytime except in northeasterly conditions
Current	Slight
Look for	Porcupine fish, pink sponges, girdled wrasse, crayfish

Milford Sound is 16 km long, and this dive site is located on the southern side of the entrance to the fiord, where it meets the Tasman Sea. It is the closest to open sea diving you will experience in Fiordland. The freshwater layer is minimal, so there is more light underwater and the sea appears bluer. Milford Sound has a maximum depth of 290 m, but the junction with the Tasman Sea is just 120 m deep.

Entering the water, you find yourself in a vast landscape, hovering over a large and colourful boulder field covered in bright green rimu weed that extends to 16–20 m. Almost immediately, girdled wrasse will start buzzing around you. By the end of the dive, you'll think they are as annoying as the sandflies above water. As you swim further into Milford Sound, with the land on your right, you come to a wall that drops away with deep vertical cracks and overhangs. Taking advantage of the lower light conditions are huge colonies of yellow zoanthids and unusual pink finger sponges. Giant slabs of rock with huge and long narrow cracks abound. Peer into a crack and it is likely many pairs of tiny black eyes of crayfish will be staring back. Black coral, so prominent in most of Fiordland, is not a major feature of this dive site. But expect to see plenty of invertebrate life, and some interesting sea fishes, including scarlet wrasse, porcupine fish, dogfish and the ever-annoying girdled wrasse.

Cook's Garden

Location	Anchor Island, Dusky Sound
Access	Boat
Type of dive	Wall and boulder bottom
Level	Open water
Snorkel	No
Depth range	0–30 m
When to dive	Anytime
Current	Slight
Look for	Tube anemones, sea spiders, octopus, nudibranchs

This is a very colourful dive. Start on the west side of Anchor Island in a brown, green and red seaweed garden. It is a remarkably pretty and inviting dive that begins quite flat but, as you descend, the shallow, bright green algae give way to the bristly rimu weed. Once you get to about 18 m, sandy patches start to appear, as well as tube anemones, sweeping through the current with their long tentacles. Soon after this, the typically steep Fiordland wall begins. This wall is particularly precipitous –the water is over 100 m deep within 200 m of the shoreline. Black coral trees appear at a depth of around 20 m. This is an impressive underwater environment, where many interesting species make their home. As well as the ever-present schools of butterfly perch, look for large schools of telescope fish. Save time and air for a safety stop in the shallows. You'll find lots of large anemones and plenty of other invertebrate animals, including seas stars, octopus, nudibranchs and sea spiders.

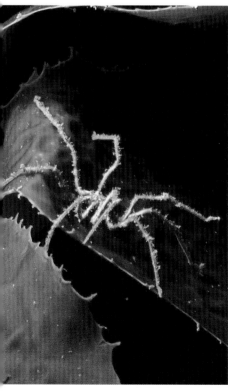

Cook's Garden

Abbo's Rocks

Abbo's Rocks

Location	Anchor Island, Dusky Sound
Access	Boat
Type of dive	Boulder bottom
Level	Open water
Snorkel	No
Depth range	0–30 m
When to dive	Anytime
Current	None
Look for	Trumpeters, copper moki, crayfish, interesting underwater geology

As the name suggests, this is an interesting dive on some seriously huge boulders. They look like a pile of fallen building blocks, scattered on top of and beside one another, creating an interesting underwater structure in the middle of the bay off the northern side of Anchor Island. The boulders are covered in life: kelp clings to the upper surface; bryozoans to the sides. Because the underwater topography in Fiordland is mostly steep walls that quite quickly fall beyond the usual habitable depths, this type of terrain is a natural magnet for fish, its cracks, holes and spaces providing refuge. Not only are the fish abundant and varied – butterfish, leatherjackets, marblefish, blue and copper moki, girdled wrasses – they are huge.

Imagine, if you will, a single kina 25 cm across. If you had to have a dive site named after you – in this case after Richard 'Abbo' Abernethy, a local dive-charter operator – then this one would not disappoint.

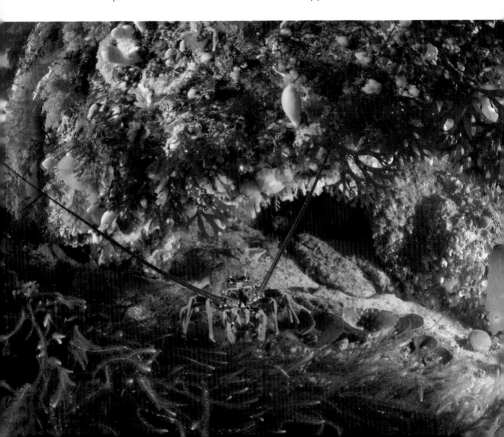

The Waikare

In 1910, 141 passengers and 85 crew were enjoying the outstanding scenery of Dusky Sound when their ship, SS *Waikare*, struck an uncharted rock between Indian Island and Passage Inlet. The crew safely landed all of the passengers, but the ship was damaged beyond repair. It managed to limp to a beach on nearby Stop Island, where the crew salvaged as much as possible before the ship eventually sank. The remaining parts of the dishevelled wreck sit in 8–20 m, and a century underwater has left it broken and rusty, but alive with colour and fish life.

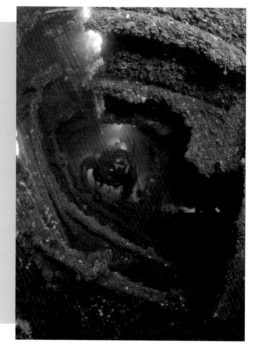

Shag Point

Location	Anchor Island, Dusky Sound
Access	Boat
Type of dive	Wall
Level	Open water
Snorkel	No
Depth range	0–30 m
When to dive	Anytime, but best when there is at least some current
Current	Moderate
Look for	Lots of fish, telescope fish, large black coral trees

This dive starts out like many typical wall dives in Fiordland – the life-encrusted wall drops off steeply to 30 m or so. Before you get very far, you'll find that not only is the wall a colourful display of invertebrate life, it is also home to many fish. Look for scorpion fish and Jock Stewarts (sea perch) resting on the wall, and ornate little nudibranchs clinging to hydroid trees. The dense schooling fish life will swim up to meet you from a depth of about 6–10 m. A gentle current sweeps past the island's edge and, within the stream of water, you'll find blue and copper moki and thousands of telescope fish buzzing around. At about 10 m, is one of the largest black coral trees you'll ever see: it extends more 4 m straight out from the wall into the sea. Such a large outcrop attracts and supports a community all of its own: trumpeters and blue moki swim around the white feathery branches; groups of butterfly perch and scarlet wrasses hover nearby; while ever-present girdled wrasses dash around.

Sandflies

Fiordland's sandflies are as legendary as its black coral trees. Stand still for more than a few seconds and you will be attacked by these tiny, yet ferocious, black flies. Their bite is not so bad, but the remnant – an itchy, red welt – will leave you frankly annoyed. According to Maori legend, after the final sculpting of Milford Sound, the goddess of death, Hine-nui-te-po, released the sandflies to keep people moving and prevent them becoming idle, enthralled by the magnificent view. It works.

Species identification guide

Fish

Schooling fish

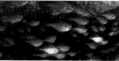

Big eye
Pempheris adspersa

Blue maomao
Scorpis violaceus
Maomao

Butterfly perch
Caesioperca lepidoptera
Oia

Golden Snapper
Centroberyx affinis
Koarea

Jack mackerel
Trachurus novaezelandiae
Hauture

Koheru
Decapterus koheru
Koheru

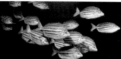

Mado
Atypichthys latus

Oblique-swimming triplefin
Obliquichthys maryannae

Parore
Girella tricuspidata

Pink maomao
Caprodon longimanus
Matata

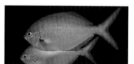

Sweep
Scorpis lineolatus
Hui

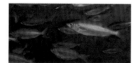

Telescopefish
Mendosoma lineatum
Koihi

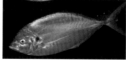

Trevally
Pseudocaranx dentex
Arara

Two-spot demoiselle
Chromis dispilus

Yellow-eyed mullet
Aldrichetta forsteri
Aua

Open water fish

Kahawai
Arripis trutta
Kahawai

Kingfish
Seriola lalandi
Haku

Spiny dogfish
Squalus acanthias

Bronze whaler shark
Carcharhinus brachyurus
Horopekapeka

Mako shark
Isurus oxyrinchus
Mango

Around the kelp

Butterfish (Greenbone)
Odax pullus
Marari/oeaea

Green wrasse (male)
Notolabrus inscriptus

Green wrasse (female)
Notolabrus inscriptus

Banded wrasse
Notolabrus fucicola
Tangahangaha

Silver drummer
Kyphosus sydneyanus

Clown toado pufferfish
Canthigaster callisterna

Topknot
Notoclinus fenestratus

Sea horse
Hippocampus abdominalis
Manaia

Spiny sea dragon
Solegnathus spinosissimus

Reef and wall dwellers

Crested blenny
Parablennius laticlavius

Common triplefin
Forsterygion lapillum

Blue-dot triplefin
Notoclinops caerulepunctus

Blue-eyed triplefin
Notoclinops segmentatus

Mottled triplefin
Grahamina capito

Spectacled triplefin
Ruanoho whero
Ruanoho whero

166

Variable triplefin
Forsterygion varium

Yaldwyn's triplefin
Notoclinops yaldwyni

Yellow-black triplefin
Forsterygion flavonigrum

John Dory
Zeus faber
Kuparu

Northern scorpion fish
Scorpaena cardinalis
Matuawhapuku

Dwarf scorpion fish
Scorpaena papillosus

Sea perch/Jock Stewart
Helicolenus percoides
Pohuiakaroa

Toadstool grouper
Trachypoma macracanthus

Spotted black grouper
Epinephelus daemelii

Yellow-banded perch
Acanthistius cinctus

Half-banded perch
Hypoplectrodes sp

Splendid perch
Callanthias australis

Colin Gans

Bluefish
Girella cyanea
Korokoropounamu

Lord Howe coralfish
Amphichaetodon howensis

Long-finned boarfish
Zanclistius elevatus

Black angelfish
Parma alboscapularis

Hiwihiwi (kelpfish)
Chironemus marmoratus

Red Moki
Cheilodactylus spectabilis
Nanua

Painted Moki
Cheilodactylus ephippium

Copper Moki
Latridopsis forsteri

Blue Moki
Latridopsis ciliaris

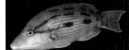

Trumpeter	Red pigfish (female)	Red pigfish (male)
Latris lineata	*Bodianus unimaculatus*	*Bodianus unimaculatus*
Kohikohi	Pakurakura	Pakurakura

Sandager's wrasse
(male & female)
Coris sandageri

Girdled wrasse
Notolabrus cinctus

Spotty
Notolabrus celiodotus
Paketi/Pakirikiri

Scarlet wrasse
Pseudolabrus miles
Puwaiwhakarua

Leatherjacket
Parika scaber
Kokiri

Porcupine pufferfish
Allomcterus jaculiferus
Koputotara

Eels

Conger eel
Conger verreauxi
Ngoiro

Short-finned eel
Anguilla australis

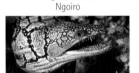
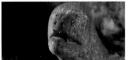

Grey moray eel
Gymnothorax nubilus

Mosaic moray eel
Enchelycore ramosa

Speckled moray
Gymnothorax obesus

Bottom dwellers

Yellow moray eel
Gymnothorax prasinus
Puharakeke

Red cod
Pseudophycis bachus
Hoka

Southern bastard cod
Pseudophycis barbata

Hapuku
Polyprion oxygeneios
Hapuku

Red-lined perch
Lepidoperca tasmanica

Goatfish (Red mullet)
Upeneichthys lineatus
Ahuruhuru

Giant boarfish
Paristiopterus labiosus

Marblefish
Aplodactylus arctidens
Kehe

Porae
Nemadactylus douglasii

Tarakihi
Nemedactylus macropterus

Snapper
Pagrus auratus
Tamure

Thornfish
Bovichtus variegatus

Giant stargazer
Kathetostoma giganteum

Blue cod
Parapercis colias
Pakirikiri/Rawaru

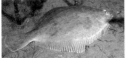

Sand flounder
Rhombosolea plebeia
Patiki

Witch flounder
Arnoglossus scapha

Short-tailed stingray
Dasyatis brevicaudata
Whai

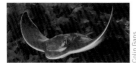

Eagle ray
Myliobatis tenuicaudatus
Whai keo

Colin Gans

Invertebrates

Clown nudibranch
Ceratosoma amoena

Flame nudibranch
Janolus ignis

Jason nudibranch
Jason mirabilis

Green nudibranch
Tambja affinis

Variable nudibranch
Alphelodoris luctuosa

Verco's nudibranch
Tambja verconis

Anemone
Bunodactis chrysobathys

Anemone
Oulactis muscosa

Dahlia anemone
Bunodactis sp

Jewel anemone
Corynactis haddoni

Red waratah anemone
Isactinia tenebrosa

Tube anemone
Cerianthus bollonsi

Wandering anemone
Phylectenactis tuberculosa

White anemone
Actinothoe albocineta

Zoanthids
Parazoanthus sp

Biscuit star
Asterodon sp

Brittle snakestars
Pectinura maculata

Snakestar (striped) & (yellow)
Astrobrachion contrictum

Firebrick sea star
Asterodiscides truncatus

Orange sea star
Henrica sp

Seastar
Asterodon miliaris

Seastar-combstar
Astropecten polyacanthus

Seven-armed sea star
Astrotole scabra

Spiny eleven arm sea star
Coscinasterias muricata

Kina/Common sea urchin
Evechinus chloroticus

Purple sea urchin
Centostephanus rodgersii

White sea urchin
Pseudechinus huttoni

White spined sea urchin
Tripneustes gratilla

Diadema sea urchin
Diadema palmeri

Sea cucumber
Stichopus mollis

Black coral (close-up)
Antipathes fiordensis

Cup coral
Monomyces rubrum

Soft coral-orange
Alcyonium aurantiacum

Pink gorgonian
Primnoa sp

Red hydracoral
Errina novaezelandiae

Sea pen
Sarcoptilus bollansi

Yellow golf ball sponge
Tethya fastigata

Flask sponge
Leucettus lancifer

Finger sponge
Lophon proximum

Finger sponge
Raspailia topseni

Sponge
Callyspongia ramosa

Sponge
Callyspongia latituba

Ascidian flask
Hypsistozoa fasmeriana

Ascidian
Didemnum densum

Sea tulips
Pyura pachydermatina

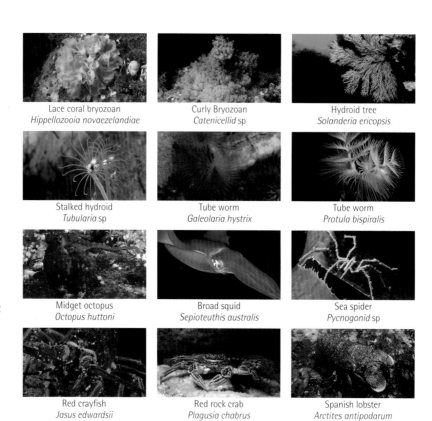

Lace coral bryozoan *Hippellozooia novaezelandiae*	Curly Bryozoan *Catenicellid* sp	Hydroid tree *Solanderia ericopsis*
Stalked hydroid *Tubularia* sp	Tube worm *Galeolaria hystrix*	Tube worm *Protula bispiralis*
Midget octopus *Octopus huttoni*	Broad squid *Sepioteuthis australis*	Sea spider *Pycnogonid* sp
Red crayfish *Jasus edwardsii*	Red rock crab *Plagusia chabrus*	Spanish lobster *Arctites antipodarum*

Algae

Ecklonia kelp *Ecklonia radiata*	Flapjack seaweed *Carpophyllum maschalocarpum*	Giant kelp *Macrocystis pyrifera*
Rimu weed *Caulerpa brownii*	Sea lettuce *Ulva* sp	Strap kelp *Lessonia variegata*

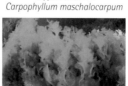

Dive operators

Northland

Cavalli Islands, *Rainbow Warrior*,
Bay of Islands, *Canterbury*

Paihia Dive HQ, Williams Road
Paihia, Bay of Islands
www.divenz.com
Telephone: +64 9 4027551

Poor Knights Islands, *Tui*, *Waikato*

Dive Tutukaka/Poor Knights Dive Centre
Marina Road, Tutukaka
www.diving.co.nz
Telephone: +64 9 4343867

The Hauraki Gulf

Hen and Chickens, Mokohinaus, Great
Barrier Island, Little Barrier Island

Goat Island Dive
Outer Gulf Charters
142a Pakiri Road, Leigh
www.goatislanddive.co.nz
Telephone: +64 9 4226925
Freephone: 0800 348369

East Coast and Bay of Plenty

White Island

Dive White/Sportsworld Whakatane
186 The Strand, Whakatane
www.divewhite.co.nz
Phone: +64 7 3070714
Freephone: 0800 DIVE WHITE

Alderman Islands

Tairua Dive
The Esplande, Tairua
www.divetairua.co.nz
Telephone: +64 7 8648054

Cook Strait

Wellington, South Coast

Island Bay Divers
353 The Parade, Island Bay, Wellington
www.ibdivers.co.nz
Telephone: +64 4 3836778

Kapiti Island

Kapiti Underwater Club
PO Box 1578 , Paraparaumu Beach
www.divekapiti.org.nz

Marlborough Sounds, *Lermontov*
wreck

Dive Picton
Corner London Quay & Auckland streets,
Picton
www.divepicton.co.nz
Telephone: +64 3 5737323

Lower South Island and Stewart Island

Stewart Island

Southern Aqua Adventures
16-18 Gore Street, Bluff
www.southernaqua.co.nz
Telephone: +64 3 2127757
Freephone: 0800 829254

Otago

Dive Otago
2 Wharf St, Dunedin
www.diveotago.co.nz
Telephone: +64 3 4664370

Fiordland

Milford Sound

Tawaki Adventures
PO Box 100, Bluff
www.tawakidive.co.nz
Telephone: +64 3 2127757
Freephone: 0800 TAWAKI

Doubtful & Dusky sounds

Fiordland Expeditions
PO Box 300, Te Anau

www.fiordlandexpeditions.co.nz
Telephone: +64 3 2499005
Freephone: 0508 TUTOKO

Dive expeditions

Dive T.E.C / Pete Mesley Expeditions
Specialised trips for experienced and
technical divers. Frequent trips to the
Lermontov and other New Zealand wrecks.
www.petemesley.com
Telephone: +64 27 2782250

Websites

Gillian and Darryl Torckler
www.torckler.com

New Zealand on the web
www.nz.com

Tourism New Zealand
www.newzealand.com

NZ Department of Conservation
www.doc.govt.nz
*follow links for information about
marine reserves*

Further reading

Andrew, N and Francis, M. 2003. *The Living Reef: The Ecology of New Zealand's Rocky Reefs*. Craig Potton Publishing, Nelson.

Enderby, J & T. 2006. *A Guide to New Zealand's Marine Reserves*. New Holland, Auckland.

Francis, M. 2001. *Coastal Fishes of New Zealand* (Third Edition). Reed Publishing, Auckland.

Torckler, G & D. 1999. *Underwater Wonders of New Zealand*. New Holland, Auckland.

Torckler, G & D. 2003. *Life-size Guide to New Zealand Fish*. Random House, Auckland.

Index

For specific dive-site information, please refer to the table of contents.

About the authors

Since the publication of their first book in 1999, Gillian and Darryl Torckler have used their combined passion for the sea, and Darryl's exquisite natural history photography, to introduce many readers to the hidden underwater world of New Zealand. Darryl's is world renowned for outdoor and underwater photography, leading to dozens of awards, magazine features and books, including ten that he has co-authored with his wife, Gillian Torckler. Between them, they have close to 60 years of diving experience and they have dived in almost every ocean. Together, they have swum with whales, dolphins and sharks; and explored the Pacific Ocean widely. For *Top New Zealand Dive Sites*, they have visited and documented the very best of New Zealand's many diving areas.

Acknowledgements

We are grateful to the many people who assisted and supported us as we researched and prepared this book. It is not possible to mention every single person, but we would like to thank the following people for their assistance with diving and access to locations: Tim Walshe (Island Bay Dive, Wellington); Mike and Janine Haines (Tawaki Dive, Milford Sound and Southern Aqua Adventures, Stewart Island); Richard and Mandy Abernethy (Fiordland Expeditions, Manapouri); Dave Watson and Nathan Winter (Otago Dive, Dunedin); Ben and Dale Ashworth (Dive Picton, Picton); Ben and Sara Knight (Kapiti); Aaron Sherin and Terry Thompson (Kapiti Underwater Club, Kapiti); Dave and Donna Earley (Tairua Dive, Tairua); Tony Bonne and Louise Bonne (Dive White, Whakatane); Gary Ball (Whakatane); Kate Malcolm and Luke Howe (Dive Tutukaka, Tutukaka); Kelly Weeds and Ty White (Paihia Dive HQ, Paihia); Brian, Chris and Julie George (Goat Island Dive, Leigh).

In addition, we would like to especially thank Dr Steve Cook and Dr Malcolm Francis for invertebrate and fish identification, respectively; Jason Hosking, and Rob and Sue Lile for support; and Pete Mesley and Colin Gans for kindly allowing us to use some of their photographs.

We are indebted to our agent, Glenys Bean, for her drive and management; the team at Penguin Books (Gillian Tewsley and Jeremy Sherlock) for their patience and vision; and Graeme Leather for his expert copy-editing and design.

Lastly, we must acknowledge our very patient children, Matthew and Ryan, who make their own sacrifices each time we embark on a project such as this.